YORK NOTES

D0256350

FRANKENSTEIN

MARY SHELLEY

**NOTES BY ALEXANDER FAIRBAIRN-DIXON
REVISED BY EMMA PAGE**

PEARSON

YORK PRESS

YORK PRESS
322 Old Brompton Road, London SW5 9JH

PEARSON EDUCATION LIMITED
Edinburgh Gate, Harlow,
Essex CM20 2JE, United Kingdom

Associated companies, branches and representatives throughout the world

First published 1999
New edition 2003
This new and fully revised edition 2015

10 9 8 7

ISBN 978–1–4479–8214–2

Illustrated by Rob Foote
Typeset by DTP Media
Printed in Malaysia (CTP-PJB)

Photo credits: Popova Valeriya/Shutterstock for page 8 top / Triff/Shutterstock for page 10 top / © iStock/MisoKnitl for page 12 bottom / Purestock/Thinkstock for page 13 top / Milosz_M/Shutterstock for page 16 top / © iStock/© James Carroll for page 16 bottom / © iStock/io_nia for page 19 middle / manfredxy/ Thinkstock for page 20 top / EggHeadPhoto/Shutterstock for page 21 bottom / © iStock/© Erin Cadigan for page 22 bottom / Creatas/Thinkstock for page 25 bottom / © iStock/gaiamoments for page 27 bottom / CHEN MIN CHUN/ Shutterstock for page 29 bottom / nito/Shutterstock for page 30 top / Dr.G/ Shutterstock for page 35 top / © iStock/Stocksnapper for page 37 top / © iStock/ northlightimages for page 40 bottom / © iStock/Yuri for page 43 bottom / Andreas Weber/Thinkstock for page 45 bottom / © iStock/Wingmar for page 50 middle / Denis Burdin/Shutterstock for page 52 bottom / © iStock/Juanmonino for page 54 bottom / Hemis/Alamy for page 56 bottom / Vicki Beaver/Alamy for page 57 bottom / Kutlayev Dmitry/Shutterstock for page 58 bottom / Ase/ Shutterstock for page 62 / © iStock/GoranStimac for page 66 top / Outdoor- Archiv/Schneider/Alamy for page 67 bottom / GL Archive/Alamy for page 68 top / Alfio Scisetti/Alamy for page 72 bottom / John Panella/Thinkstock for page 74 bottom / ZHARATE/Thinkstock for page 75 top / DenisNata/Shutterstock for page 76 middle / wavebreakmedia/Shutterstock for page 79 middle

CONTENTS

PART FOUR:
THEMES, CONTEXTS AND SETTINGS

PART FIVE:
FORM, STRUCTURE AND LANGUAGE

PART SIX:
PROGRESS BOOSTER ★

PART SEVEN:
FURTHER STUDY AND ANSWERS

PREPARING FOR ASSESSMENT

HOW WILL I BE ASSESSED ON MY WORK ON *FRANKENSTEIN*?

All exam boards are different, but whichever course you are following, your work will be examined through these four Assessment Objectives:

Assessment Objectives	Wording	Worth thinking about ...
AO1	Read, understand and respond to texts. Students should be able to: • maintain a critical style and develop an informed personal response • use textual references, including quotations, to support and illustrate interpretations.	• How well do I know what happens, what people say, do etc.? • What do I think about the key ideas in the novel? • How can I support my viewpoint in a really convincing way? • What are the best quotations to use and when should I use them?
AO2	Analyse the language, form and structure used by a writer to create meanings and effects, using relevant subject terminology where appropriate.	• What specific things does the writer 'do'? What choices has Shelley made (why this particular word, phrase or paragraph here? Why does this event happen at this point?) • What effects do these choices create – suspense? Sympathy? Horror?
AO3	Show understanding of the relationships between texts and the contexts in which they were written.	• What can I learn about society from the play? (What does it tell me about justice and prejudice, for example?) • What was society like in Shelley's time? Can I see it reflected in the novel?
AO4	Use a range of vocabulary and sentence structures for clarity, purpose and effect, with accurate spelling and punctuation.	• How accurately and clearly do I write? • Are there small errors of grammar, spelling and punctuation I can get rid of?

Look out for the Assessment Objective labels throughout your York Notes Study Guide – these will help to focus your study and revision!

The text used in these Notes is the Penguin Classics edition 2003.

HOW TO USE YOUR YORK NOTES STUDY GUIDE

You are probably wondering what is the best and most efficient way to use your York Notes Study Guide on *Frankenstein*. Here are three possibilities:

A **step-by-step** study and revision guide	A **'dip-in'** support when you need it	A **revision guide** after you have finished the novel
Step 1: Read Part Two as you read the novel, as a companion to help you study it. **Step 2:** When you need to, turn to Parts Three to Five to focus your learning. **Step 3**: Then, when you have finished, use Parts Six and Seven to hone your exam skills, revise and practise for the exam.	Perhaps you know the book quite well, but you want to check your understanding and practise your exam skills? Just look for the section you think you need most help with and go for it!	You might want to use the Notes after you have finished your study, using Parts Two to Five to check over what you have learned, and then work through Parts Six and Seven in the immediate weeks leading up to your exam.

HOW WILL THE GUIDE HELP YOU STUDY AND REVISE?

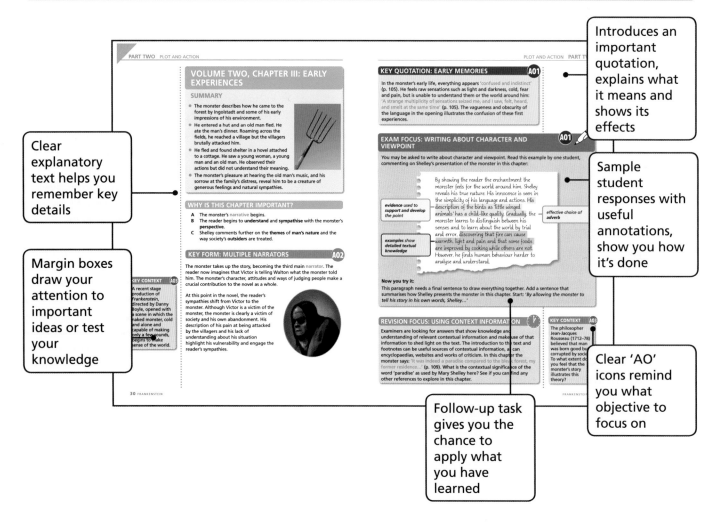

Clear explanatory text helps you remember key details

Margin boxes draw your attention to important ideas or test your knowledge

Introduces an important quotation, explains what it means and shows its effects

Sample student responses with useful annotations, show you how it's done

Follow-up task gives you the chance to apply what you have learned

Clear 'AO' icons remind you what objective to focus on

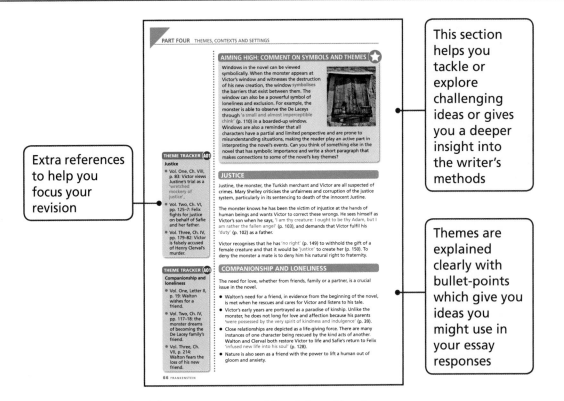

Extra references to help you focus your revision

This section helps you tackle or explore challenging ideas or gives you a deeper insight into the writer's methods

Themes are explained clearly with bullet-points which give you ideas you might use in your essay responses

Finally, Parts Two to Five end with a **Progress and Revision Check**:

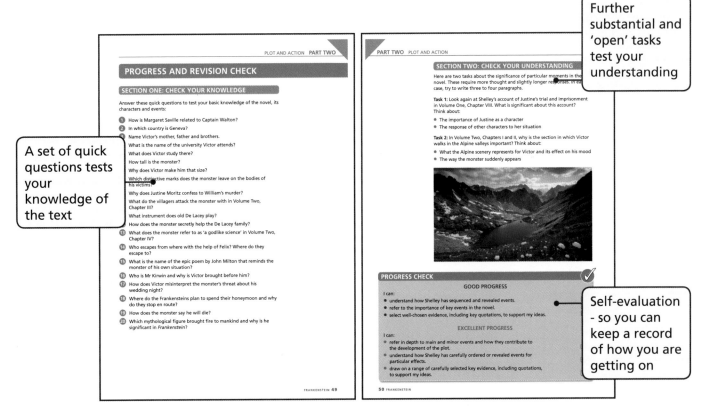

A set of quick questions tests your knowledge of the text

Further substantial and 'open' tasks test your understanding

Self-evaluation - so you can keep a record of how you are getting on

Don't forget Parts Six and Seven, with advice and practice on **improving your writing skills**:

● Focus on **difficult areas** such as **'context'** and **'inferences'**

● **Short snippets** of **other students' work** to show you how it's done (or not done!)

● Three annotated **sample responses** to a task **at different levels**, with **expert comments**, to help you judge your own level

● **Practice questions**

● **Answers** to the **Progress and Revision Checks** and **Checkpoint** margin boxes

Now it's up to you! Don't forget – there's even more help on our website with more sample answers, essay planners and even online tutorials. Go to **www.yorknotes.com** to find out more.

PLOT SUMMARY: WHAT HAPPENS IN *FRANKENSTEIN*?

WALTON'S STORY (VOLUME ONE, LETTERS I–IV)

- Captain Robert Walton is on a dangerous voyage to the North Pole when his ship becomes icebound.
- While he is stuck, he sees a 'gigantic' (p. 25) being on a sledge. Walton then discovers Victor Frankenstein on the brink of death.
- Walton looks after Victor who begins to tell him his story.

VICTOR'S STORY (VOLUME ONE, CHAPTER I TO VOLUME TWO, CHAPTER II)

- Victor grew up with an orphan named Elizabeth whom his mother had adopted.
- At university he is inspired by a scientist, M. Waldman. Victor hopes that science will provide him with the key to creating life itself.
- Obsessively, he digs up corpses and uses them to build a gigantic man, to whom he hopes to give life. He succeeds, but is devastated by its ugliness and runs away from it in horror. Victor becomes unwell.
- The monster disappears and Victor is nursed back to health by his friend Clerval.
- Victor receives a letter from his father, Alphonse, telling him that his brother, William, has been murdered. Victor journeys home to Geneva.
- On the way, Victor sees the monster amidst the Alps and becomes convinced that the monster is William's murderer.
- When he meets his family, Victor learns that Justine, their servant, has been accused of the murder. Although innocent, Justine confesses and is hanged.
- Unable to tell his family about the monster, Victor spends his time alone. He travels into the Alps where he meets the monster. He wants to kill him, but the monster reproaches him. Victor feels 'the duties of a creator towards his creature' (p.104) and the monster begins to tell his tale.

THE MONSTER'S STORY (VOLUME TWO, CHAPTERS III–VIII)

- The monster tells Victor about 'the original era' (p. 105) of his life as he gradually learned about the world. He tried to express himself but the sounds he made were 'uncouth and inarticulate' (p. 106).
- He wandered into a village and was attacked, so fled to the country.
- The monster hid and observed the daily life of a poor family called the De Laceys. He was moved by the kindness of the son and daughter to their old, blind father.
- When a young Arabian girl called Safie arrived, the son, Felix, taught her his language. From his hovel, the monster also learned to speak and read.

KEY CONTEXT **A03**

In 1816 Mary Shelley was staying at the poet Byron's Villa Diodati by Lake Geneva in Switzerland. Byron challenged each person present to write a ghost story and this inspired Shelley with the idea for *Frankenstein*.

TOP TIP **A01**

Frankenstein's creation does not have a name. He is referred to in this guide as 'the monster' and you can do the same in your exam. Keep track of some of the other ways Victor refers to his creation, e.g. 'daemon' and 'fiend' and consider the connotations of these words.

- One day when the blind man was alone, the monster introduced himself. The family returned and Felix pushed the monster to the ground and beat him with a stick.
- In anguish, the monster fled and decided to find his creator. On the way he saved a young girl from drowning but was shot by a peasant.
- He tried to befriend a young boy, William. The boy rejected him and revealed that he was a Frankenstein. The monster strangled the William and placed a portrait the boy was wearing in the dress of a girl (Justine) as she slept.
- Finally, the monster explains that his misery and loneliness have made him act badly. He asks Victor to create a female companion for him.

KEY CONTEXT A03

Shelley quotes from William Wordsworth's poem 'Tintern Abbey' (p. 161) – one of the most famous poems in English Romantic literature – to describe Clerval's love of nature.

VICTOR'S STORY CONTINUES (VOLUME TWO, CHAPTER IX TO VOLUME THREE, CHAPTER VII)

- Victor finally agrees to create a female for the monster. Victor's father proposes that Victor marry Elizabeth. Victor agrees that he will after he has taken a tour of Britain with Clerval.
- In the Orkney Islands Victor parts with his friend and rents a hut where he can make the female monster. However, when he sees the monster at the window, he furiously tears the half-finished creature to pieces. The monster, in despair, leaves him with the words, '*I will be with you on your wedding-night*' (p. 173).
- The monster murders Clerval and makes it look as though Victor did it. Victor spends time in prison in a state of torment and delirium. Eventually, he is proved innocent.
- He marries Elizabeth. On their honeymoon, while Victor is out looking for the monster, the monster kills Elizabeth. Victor's father dies after hearing the news.
- Utterly alone, Victor decides to seek out the monster and kill him. He chases him and tracks him down near the North Pole, but loses him and needs to be rescued.

WALTON'S STORY CONTINUES (THE FINAL LETTERS, VOLUME THREE, CHAPTER VII)

- With the ship stuck in ice, Walton's crew threatens mutiny.
- Victor dies from exhaustion. Walton discovers the monster mourning the death of his creator. Walton calls him a hypocrite. The monster explains how he has been mistreated and misunderstood. He declares that has never received justice and the only solution is to commit suicide now his creator has gone.
- The monster jumps from the window and '*is lost in darkness*' (p. 225).

TOP TIP A02

Note that *Frankenstein* has a multiple viewpoint style of narration, with three narrators – Walton, Victor and the monster. This form, where one story is embedded inside another, is sometimes referred to as Chinese box or Russian doll narration. One effect of this is to draw the reader into the story and make its fantastical storyline seem a little more believable.

REVISION FOCUS: THE NOVEL'S FORM AND STRUCTURE

It is important that you are clear who is narrating each section and how the overall structure of the novel works. Insert sticky notes or markers into your copy of the text to help you divide it into the different narrative sections. Create a colour-coded chart to help you recall the events recounted in each narrator's section and the order in which they are told. Keep testing yourself until you know exactly what happens in each section.

VOLUME ONE, LETTER I: A VOYAGE OF DISCOVERY

SUMMARY

- Captain Robert Walton is writing to his 'dear sister' (p. 15), Margaret Saville, about his forthcoming expedition to the North Pole.
- Walton reassures his sister that his trip will be successful.
- He imagines the Pole will be a beautiful region of 'eternal light' (p. 15).
- Walton is excited by the prospect that the North Pole is unknown and undiscovered and hopes that he will be able to discover 'the secret of the magnet' (p. 16).
- He reminisces on his early years that were spent passionately reading his uncle's collection of seafaring books and poetry. Six years ago and against his father's dying wish, he decided to become a seafarer when he inherited the fortune of his cousin.
- Walton reflects that his spirits are sometimes 'depressed' (p. 17). He knows he will need to show great strength of character to maintain his own spirits and his crew's morale.
- He tells his sister about some more practical details of his voyage relating to modes of transport, the weather and suitable clothing.
- Walton says that he does not intend to sail until the end of June but cannot tell his sister when he will return.

WHY IS THIS CHAPTER IMPORTANT?

A We are introduced to **Robert Walton**, one of the main **narrators**.
B Walton's letters reveal **themes** that are central to our understanding of the whole novel.
C We see things from his **perspective** but we are also made to question his **character** and **motivation**.

KEY CHARACTER: CAPTAIN ROBERT WALTON **A01**

Walton is a passionate young man who is enthusiastic about his expedition. He has shown great determination to become a seafarer despite his father's dying wish that he should not. However, Walton himself comments that his daydreams 'want ... *keeping*' (p. 20), an artistic **metaphor** that suggests he can lack a sense of proportion and perspective.

There is also **ambiguity** about his motivation. Walton says he wants to 'benefit' (p. 16) mankind by his discoveries, but he is also clearly driven by a boyish sense of adventure and the enticements of 'glory' (p. 17).

KEY QUOTATION: WALTON'S SENSE OF PURPOSE **A02**

Walton often comments in his letters to his sister on his determination to voyage to the North Pole. He writes that 'nothing contributes so much to tranquilize the mind as a steady purpose – a point on which the soul may fix' (p. 16). Shelley's choice of the words 'steady', 'point' and 'fix', makes the reader think of the needle of a compass always pointing north because of its magnetic attraction.

CHECKPOINT 1 **A01**

What does Walton believe the North Pole will be like?

KEY CONTEXT **A03**

Compare Walton's story with the mythical character Prometheus. In the legend, Prometheus steals fire from heaven to help mankind (see **Contexts: Myths and legends**). Why do you think Shelley gave her novel the subtitle 'The Modern Prometheus'?

EXAM FOCUS: WRITING ABOUT WALTON **A01**

You may be asked to write in detail about a particular character. Read this example by one student commenting on the characterisation of Walton:

*a **well-expressed** point about Walton*

Walton's desire to turn 'the favourite dream of his early years' into a reality can be seen as either heroic or self-destructive. His 'ardent curiosity' to see the Pole 'is sufficient to conquer all fear and danger or death', revealing a courage that could be viewed as naive. Shelley shows us how Walton's ambitions as a man had their roots in the daydreams of his childhood. As a child, his imagination was carried away by his uncle's books about voyaging which later led him to 'voluntarily' experience 'cold, famine, thirst and want of sleep' as a sailor.

explanation of the writer's intentions

*apt **textual references***

Now you try it:

This paragraph needs a final sentence to draw everything together. Add one that provides a summarising comment about Walton's character. Start: '*Mary Shelley presents Walton...*'

VOLUME ONE, LETTER II: WALTON SETS SAIL

SUMMARY

- Walton describes his success in finding a ship and crew, but his 'enterprise' (p. 19) has been halted by bad weather.
- Walton feels gloomy and lonely because he needs a friend who can support him when he encounters difficulties.
- He tells Margaret about two courageous members of his crew: the English lieutenant and the master.
- He tells his sister a story about the master's generous and selfless treatment of a young Russian lady to whom he was once engaged.
- Walton concludes that, even though he is despondent, he is still eager to start his exploration.

TOP TIP (A02)

Keep track of Walton's changing moods throughout his letters and how they are revealed through the language he uses. Consider how Shelley uses sentence length and punctuation to achieve certain effects in Walton's narrative.

WHY IS THIS CHAPTER IMPORTANT?

A We learn about the progress **Walton** has made and also the reasons for the delay to his voyage.

B Mary Shelley introduces the important **themes** of **friendship** and **loneliness**.

C The reader begins to see Walton as an unreliable narrator prone to changing moods, to nagging doubts about his own **education** and **character** and to imaginative flights of fancy – 'a love for the marvellous' (p. 22).

KEY THEME: FRIENDSHIP

Walton's letter writing suggests that he needs someone with whom to share his experience and to 'repair' his 'faults' (p. 19), but his deep desire for a companion is in conflict with his desire to explore. Walton admits that his complaints are 'useless' because he is unlikely to find a friend on 'the wide ocean' (p. 20).

KEY CONTEXT (A03)

Coleridge published *The Rime of the Ancient Mariner* in 1798 about the 'strange things that befell' during a long sea voyage. Walton says that Coleridge's imaginative poem inspired his love for the ocean (pp. 21–2).

The need to have a friend is seen throughout the novel. Victor Frankenstein travels with his valued friend Clerval, and Frankenstein's monster tries to strike up friendships on several occasions but is shunned by society. Victor's refusal to create a mate for the monster prompts him to take revenge. Shelley repeatedly shows her readers the benefits of friendship and the harmful effects of loneliness and alienation.

VOLUME ONE, LETTER III: THE VOYAGE CONTINUES

SUMMARY

- Three more months have passed and Walton is nearer the Pole.
- The safety and progress of Walton's vessel are threatened by 'floating sheets of ice' and 'stiff gales' (p. 23).
- Walton plays down these dangers and is optimistic and resolute about the voyage.
- Walton continues to dream about his future 'success' (p. 23) and 'triumph' (p. 24).
- He praises his crew's courage and assures his sister he will not take unnecessary risks.

WHY IS THIS CHAPTER IMPORTANT?

A We learn about the **progress** made and the **difficulties** faced by **Walton** and his crew.

B The reader's awareness of Walton's **changing moods** and **emotional instability** grows.

KEY LANGUAGE: CONTRADICTIONS A02

Optimistic in his first letter, despondent in his second, Walton is again in 'good spirits' (p. 23) in this short third letter. Walton describes this letter as 'a few lines in haste' (p. 23) and this may in part account for its inconsistencies and contradictions. For example, the reader may find Walton's claim that the 'southern gales' give him a 'renovating warmth' (p. 23) unconvincing. Walton's desire both to persevere with his voyage and to reassure Margaret leads him to contradict himself.

AIMING HIGH: ANALYSE NARRATIVE FORM ⭐

In Mary Shelley's novel, Walton's letters to his sister can be seen as a framing narrative, providing a context and setting in which Victor Frankenstein tells the events of his life, as well as a character to whom Victor can narrate those events. In Walton's third letter, he writes that the only accidents that have occurred on this voyage are ones 'which experienced navigators scarcely remember to record' (p. 23).

Shelley seems to be preparing readers here for the extraordinary turn of events that Walton 'cannot forbear recording' (p. 25) in his fourth letter and for the incredible story that the character of Victor Frankenstein will begin to tell his astonished listener. Shelley's choice of form enables the reader to identify with Walton as he listens and reacts to Victor's 'Strange and harrowing' (p. 32) story. You will gain more marks if you explain the effects on the reader of framing the central storyline in this way. What do you think are the effects?

CHECKPOINT 2 A01

What personal qualities does Walton value in his crew?

TOP TIP A01

Walton uses emotional language at the end of the letter. He uses both rhetorical questions: 'What can stop the determined heart and resolved will of man?' (p. 24), and an exclamation: 'Heaven bless my beloved sister!' (p. 24) in the closing paragraphs.

VOLUME ONE, LETTER IV: A TROUBLED NEW FRIEND

SUMMARY

- A month later Walton's ship is stuck in the ice and surrounded 'by a very thick fog' (p. 25).
- The mist clears and Walton and his crew see a man 'of gigantic stature' (p. 25) travelling on a sledge pulled by dogs. The man disappears from sight and they are unable to follow him.
- The following morning, Walton and his crew discover another traveller, who speaks English with a foreign accent and is extremely cold and weak.
- The man agrees to come on board and Walton and his crew nurse him. They are curious about their guest.
- The guest shows great interest in the sighting of the other traveller. Despite his poor health, the man is eager to spend time on deck 'to watch for the sledge which had before appeared' (p. 28).
- Two weeks pass and Walton grows fond of his guest and feels 'admiration and pity' (p. 28) for him.
- The man agrees to tell Walton his story. Walton resolves to record the story faithfully and send the manuscript to Margaret.

WHY IS THIS CHAPTER IMPORTANT?

A The reader is introduced to **Victor Frankenstein**, the **central character**.

B Shelley gives Walton and his crew – and thus the reader – an intriguing first glimpse of **Frankenstein's monster**.

C A **friendship** between Walton and Frankenstein begins – the first of several important friendships in the novel.

D Shelley heightens the reader's interest in the strange visitor's past life and introduces his narrative in a way that builds **suspense**.

CHECKPOINT 3 **A01**

What is Walton's attitude towards Victor?

EXAM FOCUS: WRITING ABOUT EFFECTS (A04)

You may be asked to write about the effects of some of the writer's choices and techniques. Read this example by one student that comments on the effects of Shelley's choice of setting:

> The remoteness of the North Pole prepares the reader for the strange sighting of the two travellers and the tale that Frankenstein intends to tell. 'Prepare to hear of occurrences which are usually deemed marvellous' says Victor, accepting that his story would ordinarily invite 'unbelief' or 'ridicule'. This awe-inspiring wilderness is a fitting setting for the strange and dramatic events that will follow and is the first of several sublime landscapes in which the novel's events are set. Coleridge talked of the importance of the 'willing suspension of disbelief', the way in which the reader is prepared to accept the impossible in order to enjoy a story.

comments on the setting and its effect on the reader

link made to other settings in the novel

links text and literary context

Now you try it:

This paragraph needs a final sentence to link Coleridge's ideas to the paragraph as a whole. Add a sentence that explains how Shelley's choice of setting is effective even though it seems so fantastical. Start: *'The North Pole is an effective choice of setting...'*

KEY CHARACTERS: VICTOR FRANKENSTEIN AND THE MONSTER (A01)

The letters set up a contrast between Frankenstein and the monster. The creature 'had the shape of a man' but was 'gigantic' (p. 25). He seems to Walton and the crew to be 'a savage inhabitant of some undiscovered island' (p. 26). Frankenstein, meanwhile, is someone with whom the crew can communicate and develop a friendship. He is a 'European' gentleman who speaks English 'with a foreign accent' (p. 26). He is 'attractive and amiable' (p. 28) yet there is a tension between the light and dark aspects of his character. Shelley is showing the reader that although Frankenstein is 'wretched' (p. 28) and his fortunes 'wrecked' (p. 32), his humanity is very much in evidence and Walton and the reader gain insights into the kind of man he must once have been.

KEY THEME: KNOWLEDGE (A01)

The attraction of knowledge emerges as a crucial theme of the novel. Frankenstein despairs when Walton confesses that he would sacrifice his own life in order to discover the knowledge he desires. Frankenstein recognises something of himself in Walton and warns him that an extreme desire for knowledge can be dangerous.

KEY CONTEXT (A03)

Shelley directly alludes to the Bible story of Adam and Eve's expulsion from the Garden of Eden in this chapter (the 'serpent').

TOP TIP (A01)

As you read on, keep track of the idea of the pursuit of knowledge and its consequences throughout the novel.

VOLUME ONE, CHAPTER I: FRANKENSTEIN'S CHILDHOOD

SUMMARY

- Frankenstein describes his family history and childhood. We learn that Victor was born into a wealthy Swiss family famous for its involvement in law and politics.
- His father, Alphonse Frankenstein, had married Caroline Beaufort. She had been left an orphan when her father, previously a rich merchant and Alphonse's best friend, lost his wealth, became a recluse and died.
- Victor was born in Naples during his parents' travels in Italy and his early life was 'but one train of enjoyment to me' (p. 35).
- A key figure in his life is his foster sister, Elizabeth Lavenza. Caroline rescued the orphaned Elizabeth from a poor peasant family.

WHY IS THIS CHAPTER IMPORTANT?

A We learn that **Victor's childhood** was happy and loving.
B We learn of the **nurturing** and **benevolent** natures of Victor's **family** members.
C Shelley shows us the value both of good, dependable **friends** and of a stable and loving family.

KEY CHARACTER: ELIZABETH

In this chapter, Victor describes accompanying his mother to visit a peasant family and being struck immediately by the sight of Elizabeth, who 'appeared of a different stock' (p. 36). Indeed, Victor and his mother discover that Elizabeth's German mother died in childbirth and that her father was 'a Milanese nobleman' who 'exerted himself to obtain the liberty of his country' (p.36), leaving her in the care of foster parents.

Victor describes her physical beauty in detail: her hair of 'the brightest living gold', her 'clear and ample' brow and her 'cloudless' blue eyes (p. 36). Her physical attributes are seen to signify her good character and in particular her 'sensibility and sweetness' (p. 36) and Victor even uses the words 'heaven-sent' and 'celestial' to convey her angelic nature (p. 36). The effect on the reader is to present Elizabeth as a figure who will be significant in Victor's life 'till death' (p. 37) and as a person of exemplary virtue.

TOP TIP (A01)

What are the personal qualities that Frankenstein seems to admire in this chapter?

KEY THEME: THE VALUE OF GOOD PARENTING (A01)

This chapter introduces the importance to Victor of the role of parents. He sees Caroline and Alphonse as responsible parents who 'fulfilled their duties' (p. 35) towards him. His happy childhood is entirely due to their 'stores of affection' (p. 35) and kindness.

Caroline is a gentle and loving character. The language Victor uses to describe her suggests her goodness and virtue. These qualities are echoed in Elizabeth, who also embodies them.

Caroline's and Elizabeth's real fathers are seen as irresponsible, unnecessarily plunging their daughters into distress. Beaufort forces Caroline to live with him in wretched isolation out of honour and 'false pride' (p. 33). Elizabeth's father is inspired by the 'antique glory' (p. 36) of Italy and leaves her behind in order to fight for his country. Shelley is showing the reader that men are capable of pursuing goals or ideals that can be harmful both to themselves and to those close to them.

> **CHECKPOINT 4** (A01)
>
> Who was Beaufort and what is his connection to the Frankenstein family?

EXAM FOCUS: WRITING ABOUT CHARACTER (A01)

You may be asked to write about significant characters in the novel. Read this example by one student, commenting on Victor's key role as both the main narrator and the central character of Shelley's novel:

use of technical term

Victor Frankenstein is the main narrator of the novel. His wish to reveal the cause of his misfortunes, which he had originally intended to keep secret, gives the story a personal and intimate – even confessional – feeling. Victor is also the central character of his own story and his beliefs, passions and ways of judging other people are crucial to the story and to the way it is told. For example, he says about his father that 'the circumstances of his marriage illustrate his character', suggesting that he judges a person's character based on their actions and in particular their treatment of others. The reader already knows that Victor will experience some terrible misfortune in his life and is kept in suspense throughout these early chapters about what will lead to the change in his fortunes.

comments on effect

introduces evidence to illustrate prior point

explicit awareness of the reader and of the writer's effect on the reader

Now you try it:

This paragraph needs a final sentence about what we learn about Victor in these opening chapters of his narration. Start: '*Shelley chooses to have Victor narrate the events of his childhood as well as his adult life because...*'

VOLUME ONE, CHAPTER II: VICTOR'S EARLY EDUCATION

SUMMARY

- Victor describes his childhood in Geneva and compares his intellectual interests with those of Elizabeth and of Clerval.
- He writes about his close friendship with both Elizabeth and Clerval and praises their good qualities.
- A lightning strike leads to an interest in electricity and galvanism, overturning his former interest in natural history and alchemy.

WHY IS THIS CHAPTER IMPORTANT?

A   The reader learns that Victor has become fascinated with **old scientific theories** and their possibilities.

B   Victor's **adventurous** and **imaginative** friend **Henry Clerval** is introduced. He, like Victor and Captain Walton, dreams of success and glory.

KEY CONTEXT (A03)

Victor says he 'entered with the greatest diligence into the search of the philosopher's stone and the elixir of life; but the latter soon obtained my undivided attention' (p. 42). The elixir of life was a mythical potion that granted the drinker eternal life or youth. This was sometimes associated with the philosopher's stone, a substance thought to have the power to change metals into gold. Alchemists devoted themselves to making these discoveries.

KEY QUOTATION: FATE AND FOREBODING (A01)

Victor says of his passion for knowledge, 'I find it arise, like a mountain river … it became the torrent which, in its course, has swept away all my hopes and joys.' (p. 40). Victor frequently refers to his destiny in this chapter and here he uses the rather Romantic extended metaphor of a mountain river to describe how his obsession turned into his unavoidable downfall. The reader feels a sense of foreboding each time Victor reminds Walton that he has been ruined. Despite his happiness as a young man, Victor is on a path to his own 'utter and terrible destruction' (p. 43).

AIMING HIGH: THE ROLE OF READING

Being able to trace an idea across the novel as a whole is often an indication of high achievement. For example, on several occasions in *Frankenstein*, Shelley writes about the effect on various characters of reading particular books. Just as Walton's fascination for the sea was inspired by his uncle Thomas's library of seafaring books and by Coleridge's *The Rime of the Ancient Mariner*, we learn that Victor's early imagination was inspired by a book by Cornelius Agrippa, a German scholar (1486–1535) reputed to have raised people from the dead. Victor's father dismisses the volume as 'sad trash' (p. 40) but does not explain his reasoning. Victor says that had his father explained that Agrippa's ideas were outmoded, the course of his life might have been very different.

Instead, Victor continues 'to read with the greatest avidity' (p. 41) works by Paracelsus and Albertus Magnus. The more he reads, the more he becomes fascinated with immortality, eternal youth and the power to raise the dead. Victor describes himself as a 'disciple' to these thinkers (p. 41) and dreams of discovering the elixir of life. What do you think Shelley is saying about the power of books?

TOP TIP (A02)

Compare and contrast passages from the novel about books and their effects, and about the role played by teachers in guiding their pupils through the experience of reading. For example, in Volume Two, Chapter V the monster comments on the books he has learned about through Felix and Safie.

TOP TIP: WRITING ABOUT VICTOR'S EDUCATION (A01)

In writing about his own education, Victor describes himself as eager to learn although 'not to learn all things indiscriminately' (p. 39). From an early age, Victor is driven by a desire to uncover nature's 'hidden laws' (p. 38) and 'the secrets of heaven and earth' (p. 39). He compares his interests with Elizabeth's. While Elizabeth loves nature and poetry, he yearns to discover explanations for the world around him; Elizabeth loves to contemplate 'appearances', while he delights in 'investigating their causes' (p. 38).

Note that as readers we begin to see an aspect of Victor's character that could put him at risk when he is away from the moderating influence of Elizabeth and his family. He says that it was his 'temper to avoid a crowd' and to attach himself 'fervently to a few' (p. 38). Victor's 'violent' temper and 'eager desire to learn' (p. 39) would have made him 'sullen' and 'rough' (p. 40) without the calm and gentle influence of Elizabeth. This characterisation prepares us for Victor's behaviour in Volume One, Chapter IV when he is away from her.

KEY CONTEXT (A03)

Luigi Galvani (1737–98) believed that electricity was to be found in the joints and muscles of animals.

VOLUME ONE, CHAPTER III: VICTOR AT UNIVERSITY

SUMMARY

- While caring for Elizabeth, who is very ill with scarlet fever, Victor's mother dies.
- Victor attends university in Ingolstadt.
- Victor meets Professor Krempe who is scornful of the outdated texts Victor has been reading.
- A chemistry teacher called M. Waldman gives a lecture and then speaks with Victor about the wonders of modern science and – unlike Krempe – about the debt that modern science owes to men like Agrippa and Paracelsus

WHY IS THIS CHAPTER IMPORTANT?

A Victor's happy life takes a turn for the worse when he loses his mother, **Caroline**.

B Victor is inspired by his meetings with **M. Waldman** and describes these events as memorable and life changing.

KEY CONTEXT (A03)

'Natural philosophy' was the term for 'science' when *Frankenstein* was written.

CHECKPOINT 5 (A01)

What is Waldman's opinion of Victor?

KEY CHARACTER: VICTOR FRANKENSTEIN

There is a conflict between Victor's studies and his relationships with others. He feels grief over his mother's death and sadness at having to leave his family to go to university: 'I must form my own friends and be my own protector' (p. 46). However, his gloomy loneliness is relieved by the prospect of acquiring knowledge.

In this chapter the reader begins to see that Victor's enthusiasm for study has the potential to develop into an obsession: 'I felt as if my soul were grappling with a palpable enemy' (p. 49). The reader may be reminded of Goethe's character Faust, who pursues knowledge and power to an obsessive and self-destructive degree. Victor is also portrayed as having antisocial tendencies; he dislikes meeting strangers and often judges people by their physical appearance. This is seen in his contempt for M. Krempe – 'an uncouth man' (p. 47) – and his respect for M. Waldman who had 'an aspect expressive of the greatest benevolence' (p. 48). Victor's naive determination to become a 'man of science' threatens to overwhelm him.

VOLUME ONE, CHAPTERS IV AND V: BIRTH OF A MONSTER

SUMMARY

- Victor becomes withdrawn from his family and fails to visit them for two years.
- Obsessed by his scientific studies, Victor is possessed by an ambition to discover the cause of life and frantically digs up dead bodies from graveyards so that he can experiment on them.
- His health suffers, but he eventually finds a way to give life to dead matter.
- One 'dreary' (p. 58) night, the monster is born and Victor is terrified by his creation.
- The monster disappears and Victor meets Clerval, who becomes concerned about his friend's appearance and state of mind.
- Victor suffers a 'nervous fever' (p. 62) and Clerval nurses him for several months.

WHY ARE THESE CHAPTERS IMPORTANT?

A Victor becomes ever more **isolated** and ever more **obsessed** by his scientific work.

B Victor discovers **how to give life to dead matter** and begins to create a 'human being' of 'gigantic stature' (p. 54).

C From the very beginning, **the relationship between Victor and his creation** is marked by **fear**, **suspicion** and antagonism.

KEY CHARACTER: VICTOR FRANKENSTEIN (A01)

This chapter marks an important turning point in Victor's life. Initially his scientific achievements bring him 'great esteem and admiration' (p. 52). But is clear to the reader from the monster's first breath that, far from being celebrated for his contribution to science, Victor will pay a terrible price for his endeavours.

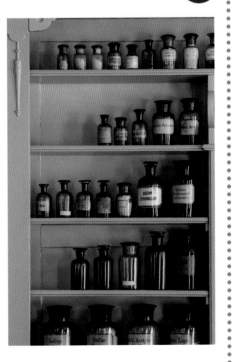

Victor despairs at the ugliness of his creation and only when it is too late and the monster has a life of its own can he see the consequences of his obsession. He abandons the creature and dreads its presence when it returns to his study. Ironically, Victor fails to experience the sense of duty towards his creation that his own parents had felt for him.

KEY CONTEXT (A03)

Before beginning *Frankenstein*, Mary Shelley and friends had been reading Coleridge's long narrative poem about a demonic stranger called 'Christabel': 'Hideous, deformed and pale of hue', 'A sight to dream of, not to tell!'

KEY CONTEXT (A03)

In Shelley's day, Prometheus was seen to symbolise man's creative striving, and his revolt against the restraints of society.

TOP TIP (A02)

The Gothic settings of the graves, churchyards, and dissecting rooms evoke an eerie atmosphere.

EXAM FOCUS: WRITING ABOUT LANGUAGE **(A02)**

You may be asked to write about the effects of Mary Shelley's language choices. Read this example by one student commenting on how Shelley writes about Victor's obsessive labours:

> Victor's isolation from society is clearly shown as a consequence of his obsession for scientific discovery, his 'one object of pursuit'. His work emaciates him, makes him oblivious to daytime and the beauty of nature, and causes him to forget his friends and family. Shelley presents Victor's behaviour as something he cannot control; his work has taken an 'irresistible hold' of him and he again appears possessed by an almighty force 'like a hurricane'. The evil nature of that force is implied by the words 'filthy' and 'profane', details that suggest Victor now thinks his experiments are morally wrong. Victor's dream in Chapter V hints at his underlying guilt. When he kisses Elizabeth she transforms into Caroline's corpse, symbolising that Victor's desires will bring destruction.

concise summary showing good **textual knowledge**

effective use of one-word quotations to highlight **language choices**

use of **semi-colon** to develop a point

fitting and effective use of **technical term**

Now you try it:

This paragraph needs a final sentence to draw everything together. Add one that summarises how Shelley's language in this section adds to the reader's unease. Start: '*In these chapters, Shelley's protagonist Victor…*'

TOP TIP **(A01)**

Victor frequently works through the night and the monster first comes to life at night time. As you read, keep track of Shelley's use of night time and particularly the moon as motifs associated with the monster throughout the novel.

CHECKPOINT 6 **(A01)**

Whose poem does Victor quote as he roams the street after creating his monster?

KEY CHARACTER: THE MONSTER **(A01)**

Victor stitches together a colossal man from the limbs of corpses. The first description of the monster is Victor's, so the physical details are described with disgust: the 'dull yellow eye', 'shrivelled complexion' and 'black lips' (p. 58). Note that Victor expresses no pride in his work and certainly no love or protective instinct towards his creation: 'the beauty of the dream vanished, and breathless horror and disgust filled my heart' (p. 58). He seems all too aware and afraid of the gigantic creature's capacity for destruction.

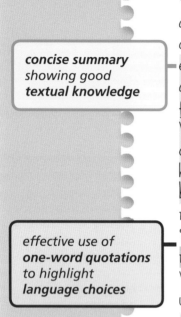

VOLUME ONE, CHAPTER VI: VICTOR'S HEALTH RECOVERS

SUMMARY

- Victor reads a letter from Elizabeth. She explains that a servant girl, Justine Moritz, has returned after some time away.
- Elizabeth also reports on the progress of Victor's younger brothers.
- Victor introduces Clerval to his professors.
- He develops a dislike for science and turns to oriental languages.
- As time passes, Victor's spirits revive.
- He takes a short tour of the countryside with Clerval

WHY IS THIS CHAPTER IMPORTANT?

A The reader learns about the welfare of Victor's household in Geneva and the return of the servant girl **Justine**.

B The outlook for **Victor** appears to be improving.

C The reader may feel, however, that Victor is seeking to **escape** his problems rather than confront them.

CHECKPOINT 7 **A01**

Is Justine merely a servant in Elizabeth's house?

KEY THEME: FAMILY LIFE **A01**

Elizabeth has replaced Caroline in the role of mother; she refers to Victor's brothers as 'our dear children' (p. 66). She continues to seek reassurance from Victor and urges him to 'Write, dearest Victor … one word will be a blessing to us' (p. 68). Her warm and loving nature is evident and the stable family life she describes contrasts with the deterioration in Victor's health.

Elizabeth also writes that Justine 'has returned to us, and I assure you I love her very tenderly' (p. 67). While Elizabeth has shown great compassion and affection towards Justine, the relationship between Justine and her mother foreshadows the relationship that will develop between the monster and Victor. Victor will feel guilty for his cruelty to the monster but will also blame him as the cause of his family's misery.

AIMING HIGH: EXPLORING CHARACTER AND MOTIVATION ⭐

Shelley uses subtle irony to invite the reader to question Victor's behaviour. It is ironic that he is tormented by the praise Waldman and Krempe give him. It is also ironic that he realises his experiments were a 'selfish pursuit' (p. 71) but fails to acknowledge that his attempt to forget the creature by pursuing other interests is equally selfish.

Victor's decision to keep the monster an unspeakable secret causes an inner conflict, a tension that becomes more acute in the chapters that follow. Could his continual delays in returning home suggest a deep-rooted guilt? You will gain more marks if you can make connections within the text, for example linking Victor's secrecy about what has happened and his repeated delays in returning to his family.

TOP TIP **A01**

Look closely at the exaggerated note of happiness and 'hilarity' (p. 72) on which this chapter ends and compare it with the sombre opening to Chapter VII. What effect do you think Shelley is aiming to achieve here?

VOLUME ONE, CHAPTER VII: JUSTINE IS ACCUSED OF MURDER

SUMMARY

- Victor learns, in a letter from his father, that his brother William has been murdered.
- In a 'painful state of mind' (p. 76), Victor slowly makes his way home to Geneva.
- Victor sees the monster in the mountains, illuminated by a 'flash of lightning' (p. 77), and believes that he is the culprit, for 'Nothing in human shape could have destroyed that fair child' (p. 78).
- Victor is overwhelmed by anguish that the being he created has proved so destructive, but feels he cannot tell anyone as they would not believe his story.
- Victor arrives at his family home to discover that Justine has been accused of the murder.

WHY IS THIS CHAPTER IMPORTANT?

A   The cheerful **tone** at the end of the previous chapter is quickly reversed when Victor learns in a letter of his brother **William's murder**.

B   The **monster** reappears and is instantly connected with the murder in Victor's mind.

C   The **themes** of **violent crime** and the workings of the **justice** system are introduced.

EXAM FOCUS: WRITING ABOUT MEANINGS AND EFFECTS (A02)

You may be asked to write about how the writer creates meanings and effects at various points in the novel. Read this example by one student, commenting on how Shelley presents Victor's complex and anguished thoughts to the reader:

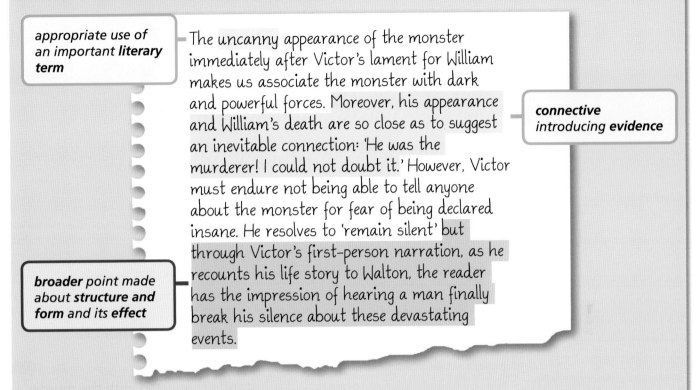

appropriate use of an important **literary term**

The uncanny appearance of the monster immediately after Victor's lament for William makes us associate the monster with dark and powerful forces. Moreover, his appearance and William's death are so close as to suggest an inevitable connection: 'He was the murderer! I could not doubt it.' However, Victor must endure not being able to tell anyone about the monster for fear of being declared insane. He resolves to 'remain silent' but through Victor's first-person narration, as he recounts his life story to Walton, the reader has the impression of hearing a man finally break his silence about these devastating events.

connective *introducing* **evidence**

broader *point made about* **structure and form** *and its effect*

Now you try it:

This paragraph needs a final sentence to draw everything together. Add one that summarises the reader's impression of Victor's complex state of mind in this chapter. Start: *'Shelley conveys to the reader...'*

KEY THEME: CRIME AND JUSTICE (A01)

This chapter introduces the themes of violent crime and the justice system. William's body is described in graphic detail, 'stretched on the grass, livid and motionless: the print of the murderer's finger was on his neck' (p. 74). Although the family's grief is immense and the loss 'irreparable' (p. 75), Alphonse's words urge his son not to respond vengefully but 'with feelings of peace and gentleness' (p. 74). Alphonse also believes in 'the justice of our laws' (p. 82) and that Justine will be acquitted if not guilty.

However, Shelley begins to cast doubt on the idea of a fair trial in various ways in this chapter. Justine was found with the valuable miniature portrait that William was carrying and her behaviour once apprehended is described as 'confused' (p. 80). Elizabeth believes everyone is 'prejudiced in so deadly a manner' (p. 82) that a guilty outcome seems very likely.

CHECKPOINT 8 (A01)

What is Alphonse's attitude towards Justine's court appearance?

TOP TIP (A01)

The missing portrait of Caroline becomes an important piece of evidence in Chapters VIII and XVI.

VOLUME ONE, CHAPTER VIII: JUSTINE IS EXECUTED

SUMMARY

- Victor blames himself for William's death.
- Justine is put on trial. She explains the circumstances but cannot explain how she came to be in possession of the miniature portrait of Caroline.
- Elizabeth makes a speech defending Justine but it backfires and Justine is condemned.
- Elizabeth and Victor visit her in prison, only to discover that the priest bullied her into a false confession. Justine is hanged.
- Victor knows the monster is the culprit and also that 'all was the work of my thrice-accursed hands' (p. 90).

WHY IS THIS CHAPTER IMPORTANT?

A The **monster** has now caused the **deaths** of two innocent people.
B Shelley is critical of the **justice** system.
C Victor suggests that his story will contain yet more **horrors**.

KEY THEME: INJUSTICE

Shelley writes about the unfairness of the legal system and corruption in religious institutions which she believed existed at the time she was writing. The judges' prejudging Justine as guilty is seen as a 'mockery of justice' (p. 83). It is a macabre **irony** that the priest should abuse his power and force Justine to falsely confess, making her feel like a 'monster' (p. 88).

The crowd is portrayed as irrational and fickle. Victor remarks that, 'all the kindness which her beauty might otherwise have excited was obliterated … by the imagination of the enormity she was supposed to have committed' (p. 83). Character witnesses are reluctant to come forward and only Elizabeth has the courage to vouch for Justine's 'excellent dispositions and irreproachable conduct' (p. 85). The public, however, see this as more evidence of Justine's guilt because of her seeming 'ingratitude' (p. 86).

KEY LANGUAGE: VICE AND VIRTUE

The religious language contrasts the virtuous Justine with the immoral Victor: Justine, a 'saintly sufferer', becomes another victim of Victor's 'unhallowed arts' (p. 90). She copes with her ordeal with remarkable dignity and composure and draws great strength from her religious faith: 'I soon shall see you again in heaven' (p. 88). Victor, by contrast, refers to himself as the 'true murderer' (p. 89) and describes himself as bearing 'a hell within me' (p. 89). Shelley is reminding the reader that although Justine loses her life, her conscience is clear while Victor – for whom the trial itself is 'living torture' (p. 83) – is to be plagued forever by the knowledge of his own wrongdoing and its grave consequences.

CHECKPOINT 9 (A01)

How do the people in court respond to Elizabeth's plea for Justine?

TOP TIP (A02)

The end of this chapter also marks the end of Volume One of Shelley's novel. How do the chapter's final two paragraphs indicate that worse horrors are to come?

VOLUME TWO, CHAPTER I: VICTOR'S REMORSE

SUMMARY

- Victor is filled with misery and guilt about Justine's death.
- His health suffers and Alphonse and Elizabeth – themselves shaken and grief stricken – are concerned about him.
- Victor senses that the monster will 'perpetrate some new wickedness' (p. 95).
- The family retire to their other home at Belrive.

WHY IS THIS CHAPTER IMPORTANT?

A Victor is ever more **isolated** by his secret.

B He begins to think about what the monster might do next and how William's and Justine's deaths can be **avenged**.

C Victor is alone in the **mountains** – a location the reader already associates with the monster.

KEY CHARACTER: VICTOR

Feeling responsible for the deaths of two innocent people, Victor experiences feelings of self-loathing. He is tempted by suicide but feels he cannot desert Elizabeth, Ernest and Alphonse and 'leave them exposed and unprotected to the malice of the fiend whom I had let loose among them' (p. 94). The reader may wonder what Victor can do to protect his family from the danger posed by the monster.

Now Victor's secret has affected the lives of others, he feels more guilty and isolated. Again, as in Ingolstadt, he 'shunned the face of man' (p. 93). Shelley describes Victor's solitude in dramatic, **Gothic** terms as 'deep, dark, deathlike' and as 'a dark cloud which brooded over me' (p. 93). Victor's woes are made worse by the fact that his loved ones cannot help as they do not know the truth; their 'good' advice, says Victor, was 'totally inapplicable to my case' (p. 94).

The way Victor contradicts himself reveals his difficulty in coming to terms with the deaths of William and Justine. Victor confesses that he 'not in deed, but in effect, was the true murderer' (p. 96) and wishes to avenge the 'crimes and malice' of the monster (p. 95). Shelley is showing the reader the complex agonies that her **protagonist** endures: hatred of the monster for his crimes combined with a sense of responsibility for the creature he brought into the world.

> **TOP TIP** A02
>
> Notice how Shelley uses satanic imagery to underscore Victor's fall into despair. He wanders like an 'evil spirit' who feels a 'hell of intense tortures' (p. 93).

> **TOP TIP** A01
>
> Compare how the Frankenstein family is described in Chapters I and II with here, following the loss of William and Justine.

VOLUME TWO, CHAPTER II: VICTOR MEETS HIS MONSTER

SUMMARY

- While journeying through the astounding Alpine scenery, Victor meets the monster in the mountains.
- Victor accuses him of murder and tries to kill him.
- The monster begs Victor for sympathy, explaining how he has suffered because Victor abandoned him.
- He implores Victor to listen to his account of events.
- They find shelter in a lonely hut and the monster begins to tell his tale.

CHECKPOINT 10 **A01**

Why does Victor let the monster tell his story?

WHY IS THIS CHAPTER IMPORTANT?

A   Victor finally comes face to face with his creation.

B   The reader is shown that despite the monster's ugly **appearance**, he possesses various **human** traits.

C   This chapter introduces the section of the novel **narrated** by the monster.

REVISION FOCUS: THE MONSTER

The monster looms large over *Frankenstein* and yet he makes relatively few appearances and his narrative forms a small section of the book. Make a list of all the monster's appearances and what we learn about him and/or Victor from each.

TOP TIP: WRITING ABOUT THE MONSTER   (A01)

It is ironic that the monster appears when Victor is feeling sorry for himself and attempting to 'forget the passing cares' (p. 100) of life. This illustrates Victor's self-deception and the dreadful and unavoidable fact of the monster's continued existence.

However, there are a number of surprises for the reader when we meet the monster. First, he does not seem to be a monster at all but a creature with very human feelings, capable of describing eloquently the reasons for his suffering: 'Everywhere I see bliss, from which I alone am irrevocably excluded' (p. 103). The reader feels sorry for his loneliness and admires his intelligence. The monster goes so far as to hint that he is 'guilty' (p. 103), showing that he has a conscience.

Second, the re-emergence in the monster's speeches of the political concerns of Chapter VIII is unexpected. He demands 'justice', 'clemency' and 'affection' from Victor (p. 103). He is able to articulate his sense of abandonment resulting from Victor's failure to take responsibility for his act of creation.

Finally, when the monster points out Victor's hypocrisy we are given an important new viewpoint on Victor's actions: 'You purpose to kill me. How dare you sport thus with life?' (p. 102). Be aware how Shelley deliberately guides the reader to be critical of Victor's perception of things.

AIMING HIGH: ANALYSE SETTING ⭐

The reader notes Shelley's portrayal of nature as an awe-inspiring and destructive power. Dramatic mountainous landscapes seized the Romantic imagination and the term sublime was coined to describe this kind of magnificent beauty. Victor describes his surroundings as 'immense', 'magnificent' (p. 97) and 'sublime' (p. 98) and finds consolation and pleasure there. However the 'terrifically desolate' scene of 'broken' and 'bent' trees and 'jutting rocks' also symbolises the wreck that Victor has become mentally and physically (p. 100).

The monster tells Victor his story in the barren and remote setting of the 'sea of ice' (p. 101) near the top of a mountain. This has much in common with the Arctic setting in which Victor tells his tale to Captain Walton, where 'mountains of ice, which admit of no escape' (p. 215) surround them. The similarities between the two settings emphasise the isolation and doom of both Victor and the monster. Can you think of other examples where Shelley's novel shows us that human endeavour is no match for the awesome power of nature? You will gain more marks if you can highlight these and make links between them.

KEY CONTEXT   (A03)

Mary Shelley includes a quotation (p. 101) from her husband's poem 'Mutability'. Of their visit to Switzerland, Percy Shelley wrote: 'I never imagined, what mountains were before.' They aroused in him: 'a sentiment of ecstatic wonder, not unallied to madness'.

VOLUME TWO, CHAPTER III: EARLY EXPERIENCES

SUMMARY

- The monster describes how he came to the forest by Ingolstadt and some of his early impressions of his environment.

- He entered a hut and an old man fled. He ate the man's dinner. Roaming across the fields, he reached a village but the villagers brutally attacked him.

- He fled and found shelter in a hovel attached to a cottage. He saw a young woman, a young man and an old man. He observed their actions but did not understand their meaning.

- The monster's pleasure at hearing the old man's music, and his sorrow at the family's distress, reveal him to be a creature of generous feelings and natural sympathies.

WHY IS THIS CHAPTER IMPORTANT?

A The monster's narrative begins.

B The reader begins to **understand** and **sympathise** with the monster's **perspective**.

C Shelley comments further on the **themes** of **man's nature** and the way society's **outsiders** are treated.

KEY FORM: MULTIPLE NARRATORS (A02)

The monster takes up the story, becoming the third main narrator. The reader now imagines that Victor is telling Walton what the monster told him. The monster's character, attitudes and ways of judging people make a crucial contribution to the novel as a whole.

> **KEY CONTEXT** (A03)
>
> A recent stage production of *Frankenstein*, directed by Danny Boyle, opened with a scene in which the naked monster, cold and alone and capable of making only a few sounds, begins to make sense of the world.

At this point in the novel, the reader's sympathies shift from Victor to the monster. Although Victor is a victim of the monster, the monster is clearly a victim of society and his own abandonment. His description of his pain at being attacked by the villagers and his lack of understanding about his situation highlight his vulnerability and engage the reader's sympathies.

KEY QUOTATION: EARLY MEMORIES (A01)

In the monster's early life, everything appears 'confused and indistinct' (p. 105). He feels raw sensations such as light and darkness, cold, fear and pain, but is unable to understand them or the world around him: 'A strange multiplicity of sensations seized me, and I saw, felt, heard, and smelt at the same time' (p. 105). The vagueness and obscurity of the language in the opening illustrates the confusion of these first experiences.

EXAM FOCUS: WRITING ABOUT CHARACTER AND VIEWPOINT (A01)

You may be asked to write about character and viewpoint. Read this example by one student, commenting on Shelley's presentation of the monster in this chapter:

> By showing the reader the enchantment the monster feels for the world around him, Shelley reveals his true nature. His innocence is seen in the simplicity of his language and actions. His description of the birds as 'little winged animals' has a child-like quality. Gradually, the monster learns to distinguish between his senses and to learn about the world by trial and error, discovering that fire can cause warmth, light and pain and that some foods are improved by cooking while others are not. However, he finds human behaviour harder to analyse and understand.

evidence *used to support and develop the point*

effective choice of adverb

examples *show detailed textual knowledge*

Now you try it:

This paragraph needs a final sentence to draw everything together. Add a sentence that summarises how Shelley presents the monster in this chapter. Start: *'By allowing the monster to tell his story in his own words, Shelley…'*

REVISION FOCUS: USING CONTEXT INFORMATION

Examiners are looking for answers that show knowledge and understanding of relevant contextual information and make use of that information to shed light on the text. The introduction to the text and footnotes can be useful sources of contextual information, as can encyclopaedias, websites and works of criticism. In this chapter the monster says: 'It was indeed a paradise compared to the bleak forest, my former residence…' (p. 109). What is the contextual significance of the word 'paradise' as used by Mary Shelley here? See if you can find any other references to explore in this chapter.

KEY CONTEXT (A03)

The philosopher Jean-Jacques Rousseau (1712–78) believed that man was born good but corrupted by society. To what extent do you feel that the monster's story illustrates this theory?

VOLUME TWO, CHAPTER IV: THE MONSTER'S EDUCATION

SUMMARY

- The monster watches the family at close quarters, trying to work out the reasons behind their behaviour.
- He is moved by the kindness the young man and woman show towards the old blind man.
- He performs acts of kindness for the family. When he finds out that their sadness is caused by poverty, he collects firewood for them in the night.
- He wants to learn language.
- Admiring the beauty of the family, the monster is mortified when he sees his own reflection in a pool in all its 'miserable deformity' (p. 117).
- He likes the family but is too frightened to join them. He hopes that in time his 'gentle demeanour and conciliating words' (p. 118) will ultimately enable him to be well received by them.

CHECKPOINT 11 (A01)

What does the monster admire in the old man?

WHY IS THIS CHAPTER IMPORTANT?

A The monster continues to watch the **De Lacey family** in the cottage.

B Shelley shows us that **friendly** and **virtuous** actions come naturally to the monster.

C This chapter focuses on the monster's **learning**, his need to explain the world around him and his hopes of being accepted into **human society**.

TOP TIP (A01)

Notice how the monster's growing interest in human beings – he 'ardently longed' (p.109) to befriend the De Laceys – contrasts with Victor's obsession with creating something inhuman from corpses.

KEY CHARACTERS: THE DE LACEYS (A01)

Notice how the monster's scientific approach to studying human beings reminds us of Victor's scientific studies. Shelley is drawing an ironic parallel between the two characters and the reasons they are interested in studying human life.

The old man and his children, Agatha and Felix, are poor 'in a very distressing degree' and often 'suffered the pangs of hunger' (p. 114). Their home is 'white-washed and clean, but very bare of furniture' (p. 110) and the monster takes refuge in a 'low hovel' (p.109) adjoining their cottage from which he observes their daily lives.

The old man's warm-hearted goodness to his family and the 'gentle manners and beauty of the cottagers' (p. 115) attract the monster, who pities them and pins all his future hopes of happiness on befriending them. He refers to 'the venerable blind father, the gentle Agatha, and the excellent Felix' (p. 117) and particularly admires the way the father encourages his children. The monster naively hopes he might be able to 'restore happiness to these deserving people' (p. 117).

EXAM FOCUS: WRITING ABOUT CHARACTER DEVELOPMENT (A02)

You may be asked to write about characterisation over the course of the novel. Read this example by one student, commenting on how Shelley shows her readers how the monster changes:

> clear **topic sentence**

Shelley presents to the reader the monster's growing interest and understanding around human beings. We see scientific language in his wish to discover 'one of the causes' behind the De Laceys' unhappiness and in his glee at making 'a discovery' about the family's use of language. Furthermore, his ambitions are emotionally charged for he 'ardently desired' and 'longed' to befriend the family. Unlike Victor, his attention and hopes are fixed on other human beings. When he finds out that the De Laceys are poverty-stricken, for example, he acts upon this knowledge by collecting firewood for them. He passionately desires to learn language and starts to pick up the basics, imagining that one day he will be able to speak to the cottagers.

> **connective phrase** introduces an interesting **contrast**

> use of a well-chosen **example to illustrate point**

Now you try it:

This paragraph needs a final sentence to draw everything together. Add a sentence that explains the effects on the reader of these developments. Start: *'Through her characterisation of the monster in this chapter, Shelley shows the reader…'*

VOLUME TWO, CHAPTER V: SAFIE'S ARRIVAL

SUMMARY

- The monster describes how the family welcomed the young Arabian woman Safie to their house.
- The monster learns more about human society and about how man 'at once so powerful, so virtuous, and magnificent' can also be 'so vicious and base' (p. 122).
- He is pained when he learns about birth, children and families because this leads him to question his own origin, parentage and present isolation.

CHECKPOINT 12 **A01**

What first impresses the monster about Safie?

WHY IS THIS CHAPTER IMPORTANT?

A   The monster observes **Safie** being welcomed into the family.
B   We learn about the forces that shape the monster's personality and the important influence of **books**.
C   The monster questions his own **origins** and **parentage**.

KEY THEMES: KNOWLEDGE, DIFFERENCE AND PREJUDICE   **A01**

KEY CONTEXT **A03**

In Volney's *Ruins of Empires* (1791), the author ponders whether electricity might be the fundamental principle of the universe.

The character of Safie is important because the De Laceys welcome her into their family without prejudice despite her difference in appearance and culture. This contrasts with the rejection the monster has experienced so far. Safie's arrival encourages him to believe that he can reveal himself to the family and be accepted. This is all the more likely because old De Lacey is blind.

As with Victor, books are an important influence on the monster and knowledge has a powerful effect on him. The more he learns about society, the less he seems to know about himself: 'I tried to dispel them, but sorrow only increased with knowledge' (p. 123). He realises that he has no money, property, family, or friends. His question, 'what was I?' (p. 123), shows a developing self-awareness of his own difference and exclusion.

REVISION FOCUS: READ A SHORT PASSAGE CLOSELY

Read the passage beginning 'It was a lady on horseback' (p. 119) and ending 'the cause of which I did not comprehend' (p. 120), which describes Safie's arrival. Make notes in the form of a spider diagram about the things that strike you about this passage, including what we learn about key characters, interesting language choices and how key themes are developed. Next, try to develop each point on your spider diagram into an extended comment. This will be good preparation for answering exam questions relating to a specific passage.

VOLUME TWO, CHAPTER VI: THE DE LACEYS' TROUBLED PAST

SUMMARY

- The monster discovers that the De Laceys are a French family whose wealth was confiscated by the authorities because Felix helped a Turkish merchant to escape from prison.
- Felix was horrified when the French law had unfairly condemned the Turk to death. As a reward for helping him to escape, the Turk promised Felix his daughter, Safie's hand in marriage.
- Felix and Safie fell in love but Felix had to return to Paris because De Lacey and Agatha had been imprisoned for their involvement in the escape. They were all banished from France.
- Safie's father did not want to honour his promise to Felix. Safie, however, ran away from her father and found the De Laceys.

WHY IS THIS CHAPTER IMPORTANT?

A The monster is moved by the **De Laceys' story**.
B He discovers why they welcomed Safie into their family.
C This **'story within a story'** reveals more about the major **characters** and develops major **themes**.

CHECKPOINT 13 **A01**

How does Safie reach safety?

AIMING HIGH: EXPLORE FORM AND THEME

At the centre of the book is another story. Although quite separate from Victor's story, the De Laceys' story links thematically to events later in the book, as well as events that have already happened. Shelley uses the De Laceys' story to explore themes that are significant throughout the novel, such as justice and injustice, exclusion and friendship, loyalty and betrayal.

For example, the persecution of the Turkish merchant by the French authorities shows the corruption of legal institutions, reminding us of Justine's mistreatment in Chapter VIII. The merchant's promise to reward Felix with his daughter, and his breaking of the promise, mirror Victor's vacillation over creating a female mate for the monster later in the novel. The Turk's 'tyrannical' (p. 129) mistreatment of Safie mirrors Victor's cruelty towards his creation in Volume Two, Chapter II and Volume Three, Chapter III. The ingratitude shown by the Turk towards Felix due to religious prejudice reflects the misplaced hatred Victor and society have towards the creature.

How would you summarise the significance of the De Laceys and their story in the novel as a whole? You will gain more marks if you can illustrate your insights with well-chosen evidence.

TOP TIP **A01**

Like Victor, Felix's ambitions and reckless actions cause the plight of his family. However, Felix battles for justice and freedom whereas Victor's final refusal to create a companion for the monster is motivated by frustration and fear rather than noble principles.

CHECKPOINT 14 **A01**

How does the monster learn of the circumstances of his creation?

KEY CONTEXT **A03**

The monster reads Goethe's *The Sorrows of Young Werther* (1774), which describes an artist's love for a girl engaged to someone else. The artist eventually commits suicide. Go to p. 69 to find out about *Paradise Lost*.

VOLUME TWO, CHAPTER VII: THE MONSTER'S EDUCATION AND SUFFERING

SUMMARY

- The monster acquires books and responds to them with great seriousness and intelligence.
- When he discovers Victor's journal, which records how he was created, he is disgusted but tries not to despair.
- He visits old De Lacey but when the rest of the family arrive they chase him out.

WHY IS THIS CHAPTER IMPORTANT?

A The monster's **understanding** of his loneliness and ugliness increases.

B He finally approaches **De Lacey** and speaks to him as he had long hoped to do.

C He is **violently** driven out of the De Laceys' home.

EXAM FOCUS: UNDERSTANDING THE RELATIONSHIP BETWEEN TEXT AND CONTEXT **A03**

You may be asked to consider the relationship between text and context in your answer. Read this example by one student, commenting on the significance of the monster's reading in this chapter:

*effective choice of **sentence structure and punctuation** to convey a complex idea*

The monster learns to love virtue and hate vice from the story of the De Laceys; however, his thoughts and feelings become more complicated as a consequence of reading. Reading Paradise Lost makes him identify his lonely state with Satan's banishment from heaven and he sometimes becomes envious of the beautiful home of the De Laceys. The hellish isolation of his hovel compared with the 'bliss' of the cottagers' paradise causes him to feel 'the bitter gall of envy'. Satan's rebellion against God is similar to the way the monster curses his creator upon finding the journal.

*draws close **connection between context and text***

*choice of phrase clearly signals **comparison***

Now you try it:

This paragraph needs a final sentence to draw everything together. Add a sentence that explains the effect of this section of the chapter on the reader's understanding of the monster's complex and changing character. Start: *'By providing the reader with insights into the monster's reading, Shelley …'*

VOLUME TWO, CHAPTER VIII: THE MONSTER AS SAVIOUR AND KILLER

SUMMARY

- The monster waits anxiously for the family to return to their cottage.
- Felix returns and tells the landlord that they are leaving their home with immediate effect.
- As night advances, the monster burns the cottage to the ground.
- The monster resolves to travel to Geneva and seek 'justice' from Victor (p. 141).
- He saves a girl from drowning and is again attacked for his kindness. Suffering both mentally and physically, his desire for revenge grows.
- After two months, he reaches Geneva. He kills William and frames Justine for the murder.

WHY IS THIS CHAPTER IMPORTANT?

A   Shelley shows how the monster's **rejection** by the De Laceys changes his **character** and **destiny**.

B   The **mood** darkens with the deepening comparisons to **Satan**.

C   The reader hears the monster's own account of the **murder** of William and the framing of Justine.

KEY LANGUAGE: THE MONSTER AS NARRATOR (A02)

Although the monster continues to present his own account of events, the character that emerges in this chapter is closer to the fiend of Victor's own descriptions. 'I, like the archfiend, bore a hell within me,' says the monster, declaring his wish to 'spread havoc and destruction' and enjoy 'the ruin' (p. 138). By his own account, the monster is portrayed as beast-like, powerful and destructive as he declares 'an ever-lasting war against the species' (p. 138). However, throughout the monster's **narrative**, Shelley presents the reader with a complex, intelligent and sympathetic character. The reader understands the desperate anguish that has led the monster to commit such despicable deeds.

TOP TIP: WRITING ABOUT THE THEME OF PREJUDICE (A01)

The monster uses the word 'unprejudiced' (p. 144) to describe William, exactly the same word he used to describe De Lacey in the previous chapter. The monster hopes that a small boy 'had lived too short a time to have imbibed a horror of deformity' (p. 144), only for those hopes to be dashed when William screams and struggles. Shelley is developing the theme of prejudice in the way both William and the 'rustic' (p. 143) instantly associate the monster's appearance and size with danger. They misunderstand his actions and intentions, as Felix, Safie and Agatha mistook his behaviour towards De Lacey. All these characters feel threatened by the monster's appearance.

TOP TIP (A01)

The monster's account finally unravels the mystery behind Caroline's portrait. The monster is attracted to Justine but this makes him feel even more isolated and frustrated. In revenge, he places the portrait in the folds of her dress.

CHECKPOINT 15 (A01)

What does the monster learn from saving the little girl?

VOLUME TWO, CHAPTER IX: THE MONSTER'S PARTING WISH

SUMMARY

- The monster wants Victor to make him a mate.
- Victor refuses, enraged by the monster's account of William's murder.
- The monster asks for sympathy and promises to 'go to the vast wilds of South America' (p. 148) and live away from mankind, in peace, if Victor grants his wish.
- Victor is 'moved' (p. 148) and changes his mind.
- Victor makes his way back to his family home but feels depressed by his promise.

TOP TIP **(A02)**

Consider how the extensive use of dialogue in this chapter gives the reader a sense of immediacy and drama.

CHECKPOINT 16 **(A01)**

Why, precisely, does the monster want a female mate?

WHY IS THIS CHAPTER IMPORTANT?

A Victor takes over the narrative for the second time.
B The monster again asks Victor to create a female companion for him.
C **Victor agrees** to the monster's request.

EXAM FOCUS: WRITING ABOUT PLOT AND CHARACTER **(A01)**

You may be asked to write about some of the author's choices about plot and character. Read this example by one student, commenting on Victor's response to the monster's request to create him a mate:

effective use of a subordinate clause at beginning of sentence

argument developed through use of connective phrase

Shelley presents to the reader Victor's considered response to the monster's request. Although Victor's immediate response is to 'refuse' him what he wants, Victor listens to the monster's arguments with compassion and believes there to be 'some justice in his argument'. On the one hand he is persuaded to create the female companion out of fear and self-preservation since the monster vows to 'revenge my injuries: if I cannot inspire love, I will cause fear.' On the other hand Victor feels guilty for abandoning the monster and wishes to 'console him'. The creature demands the female 'as a right' and Victor concludes it would be 'justice - to him and my fellow creatures' to comply.

argument developed through use of connective phrase

short memorable quotations deepen response

Now you try it:

This paragraph needs a final sentence to draw everything together. Add a sentence that considers the reader's response to the characters of Victor and the monster at this point in the novel. Start: 'The way Victor responds to the monster's request shows the reader…'

VOLUME THREE, CHAPTER I: VICTOR TRAVELS TO ENGLAND

SUMMARY

- Alphonse is concerned about his son and wishes him to marry Elizabeth at the earliest opportunity.
- Victor decides he must go away to create a mate for the monster and asks to be allowed to travel to England for a few months before the wedding.
- Victor travels with Clerval across Europe to London.
- Victor pays tribute to Clerval's excellent qualities

WHY IS THIS CHAPTER IMPORTANT?

A Victor begins to make arrangements to create a **companion** for the monster.

B Victor's **marriage** to Elizabeth is arranged.

C The reader begins to grow worried about **Clerval**'s fate.

TOP TIP (A01)

Alphonse thinks that Victor's 'gloom' (p. 156) might be because he is secretly in love with another woman. This is a powerful dramatic irony since we know that he is 'bound' by indissoluble 'ties' not to another woman but to the creature (p. 102).

EXAM FOCUS: COMMENTING ON THE WRITER'S EFFECTS (A02)

You may be asked to write about how the author builds tension and suspense. Read this example by one student, commenting on the darkening mood created by Shelley in this chapter:

explanation of how tension is created

Shelley creates tension by showing how Victor's desire to please his ageing father and honour his mother's dying wish conflicts with his plans to create another monster. He is also frustrated in his efforts by his own 'repugnance to the task' but fears the consequences of inaction. In Europe, Clerval enjoys the beautiful scenery but Victor cannot stop thinking about his promise to the monster. He worries about leaving his loved ones 'unprotected' but believes it is more likely the monster will pursue him to hold him to account. This creates suspense as to when and where the monster might appear. Shelley says Victor might eventually become liberated from his 'slavery', but the foreshadowing of Henry's death suggests that Victor's misery will only increase.

another explanation of how Shelley creates a particular effect

appropriate use of technical term

Now you try it:

This paragraph needs a final sentence to draw everything together. Add a sentence that explains the overall effect of this chapter on the reader. Start: *'Despite the fact that marriage plans are made in this chapter, the overall mood…'*

VOLUME THREE, CHAPTER II: VICTOR STARTS HIS NEW CREATION

KEY CONTEXT **A03**

Cumberland (the Lake District) was the home of the Romantic poets William Wordsworth and Samuel Taylor Coleridge.

SUMMARY

- Victor and Clerval stay in London until March. Victor begins to 'collect the materials necessary for my new creation' (p. 164).
- They travel to Edinburgh, stopping off at Windsor, Oxford, Matlock and the Cumberland lakes.
- Victor tells Clerval he wishes to make the tour of Scotland alone and travels to the remote Orkney islands to carry out his work.
- He hires a shabby hut where he starts creating the new monster. This time, he finds his work 'horrible and irksome' (p. 169)

WHY IS THIS CHAPTER IMPORTANT?

A Victor experiences rare moments of happiness on his **travels**, but always descends into misery again.

B Victor achieves the **solitude** and **secrecy** he requires and begins his work.

TOP TIP **A01**

Compare Victor's experience of creating this monster with the experience of creating the first monster in Ingolstadt in Volume One.

TOP TIP: ANALYSING LANGUAGE

It's important that you can write about some of the author's choices of language and imagery. In this chapter, Shelley shows the reader that the monster haunts Victor from every angle. The phrase 'insurmountable barrier' (p. 163) conveys a growing sense of Victor's claustrophobia. Although Victor travels a great distance during the chapter, Shelley shows us that he can neither escape the truth of past events – 'the blood of William and Justine' (p. 163) – nor the sense of being pursued by the monster now and in the future. Using metaphors, Shelley shows us that Victor is increasingly fatalistic. In Victor's description of himself as 'a blasted tree' and 'wrecked' (p. 165), the use of the adjectives 'blasted' and 'wrecked' conveys destruction and finality with great force. By the end of the chapter he is 'restless and nervous' and experiences 'obscure forebodings of evil' (p. 169) as he awaits the monster.

CHECKPOINT 17 **A01**

Why does Alphonse arrange for Clerval to go with Victor on his travels?

VOLUME THREE, CHAPTER III: A DRAMATIC TURN OF EVENTS

SUMMARY

- Victor suffers severe doubts about creating a mate for the monster.
- The monster appears and watches Victor destroy his work.
- The monster vows to take his revenge.
- Victor sails out and disposes of his unfinished creation.
- He drifts ashore on the Irish coast. Strangers surround him on the beach and take him to court in connection with a murder

WHY IS THIS CHAPTER IMPORTANT?

A   Victor's decision creates a dramatic **turning point** in the destinies of **Victor** and the **monster**.

B   The monster's **pursuit** of his creator intensifies with his haunting words 'I shall be with you on your wedding-night' (p. 173).

KEY THEMES: CREATION AND DESTRUCTION (A01)

Shelley's novel invites the reader to reflect on profound social and philosophical questions about the origins of life, the ethics of science and the responsibility of the creator towards the created. At the beginning of this chapter, Victor again contemplates the consequences of creating a mate for the monster, but this time he decides against creating another new life. He gives a number of reasons, including that 'she might become ten thousand times more malignant than her mate' and that they might propagate 'a race of devils' (p. 170). However, he takes the risk that his decision may seal his own destruction at the hands of the spurned and vengeful monster.

AIMING HIGH: EXPLORING PARALLELS BETWEEN CHARACTERS ⭐

Throughout the novel the monster notices the attractiveness of women like Safie and Justine, so asking for a mate of his own – as Victor has a mate in Elizabeth – is a natural request. To be deprived of a mate is further proof of his rejection by human society. Victor's destruction of the female is symbolic and could be seen to foreshadow Elizabeth's fate. Most female characters in the book are life-givers, whereas some of the novel's male characters can be reckless and destructive. When Victor arrives in Ireland, parallels between Victor and the monster are strengthened. Victor, as a foreigner, is not welcomed by the prejudiced and suspicious crowd. He now feels what it is to be like an innocent victim.

How does Shelley invite the reader to draw parallels between characters in her novel? You will gain more marks if you can write perceptively about the author's choice of literary techniques and their effects on the reader.

KEY CONTEXT (A03)

The lives and destinies of Victor and the monster are closely connected from the moment Victor first discovers the secret of creating life. In Danny Boyle's stage production of *Frankenstein*, two actors took it in turns to play the lead roles of Victor and the monster.

CHECKPOINT 18 (A01)

How does Victor come to land in Ireland?

VOLUME THREE, CHAPTER IV: ANOTHER MURDER TRIAL

SUMMARY

- Victor is put on trial for the murder of Clerval.
- He falls ill and spends months in prison where his father visits him.
- Eventually he is found innocent and travels home.

WHY IS THIS CHAPTER IMPORTANT?

A Victor suffers the **loss** of a dear **friend** and is falsely accused of his **murder**.

B Shelley again writes about the **themes** of injustice and imprisonment.

KEY STRUCTURE: ECHOES OF JUSTINE'S TRIAL (A02)

Forming a clear parallel with Volume One, Chapter VIII, Victor now replaces Justine as the victim on trial for murder. Witnesses come forward to give their evidence against him. He remains calm when the first man relates how he found a dead body on the beach, until he mentions that there were black fingermarks on the neck, a direct echo of the ghastly details of William's murder. Realising that his monster has done the deed, Victor almost faints. This arouses the suspicion of the magistrate, who asks Victor to look at the corpse, wanting to observe his reaction. When Clerval's body is revealed, Victor's shock arouses more suspicion. This also reminds the reader of Justine's trial when suspicion is aroused by certain misleading details (such as Justine's whereabouts and the discovery of Caroline's portrait). This trial, however, ends with the correct verdict, but not before Victor has spent two unpleasant months in prison.

KEY CONTEXT (A03)

Mary Shelley's father's book, *An Enquiry Concerning Political Justice* (1793) had greatly impressed the English Romantics, particularly Mary's husband Percy Bysshe Shelley. In his book, Godwin criticises political institutions and argues in favour of reason and against 'false opinion, superstition and prejudice' in public life.

CHECKPOINT 19 (A01)

How had the murdered man died?

TOP TIP (A01)

Victor says 'I stretched out my hand to him' (p. 185) when he sees his father. A loving and dutiful parent, Alphonse supports his son and takes him home. Compare this with Victor's treatment of the monster and with the way the monster is treated by others when he reaches out for help or even to give help.

EXAM FOCUS: COMMENTING ON THE DEVELOPMENT OF THEMES (A01)

You may be asked to write about the way the author develops key themes. Read this high-level example by one student, commenting on how Shelley uses the prison episode to develop the themes of justice and freedom:

> The themes of justice and freedom are developed as the prison takes on a symbolic role. Victor's imprisonment might remind the reader of the monster's lack of freedom in his hovel. The mental barrier Victor felt between himself and society now becomes a shocking institutional reality and he knows the complete sense of isolation that the monster has had to suffer. The 'barred windows' echo the appearance of the monster at the 'casement' - a motif Shelley uses to symbolise exclusion as well as incarceration. Victor earlier used the metaphor of 'chains' of 'iron' that had 'eaten into my flesh' but now his imprisonment is literal. In the expressions of a visiting physician and old woman, Victor sees only 'carelessness' and 'brutality', but he learns that Mr Kirwin had shown him 'extreme kindness'. The reader may compare this treatment with the mercilessness with which Justine was treated and the harshness the monster has encountered at every turn.

effective **linking** of different sections

understands that the **author** is returning to themes and creating effects **across the entire text**

appropriate use of **technical term** suggesting an understanding of the author's intentions

thoughtful comment about possible **reader response**

Now you try it:

This paragraph needs a final sentence to draw everything together. Add a sentence that comments on Shelley's apparent view of Victor and of society's treatment of the outsider in this chapter. Start: *'In this chapter, Shelley returns to the themes of justice and freedom in order to…'*

REVISION FOCUS: KEEP TRACK OF THEMES

It is worth keeping track of the novel's themes in a quick and visual way. As well as highlighting and annotating your text – perhaps using different colours to represent the novel's various themes – you could also create a colourful mind map to represent each theme as a visual reminder when you revise. Display these posters prominently to help you recall their contents. See **Themes, contexts and settings**.

VOLUME THREE, CHAPTER V: VICTOR AND ELIZABETH ARE MARRIED

SUMMARY

- Victor and his father travel to Paris.
- Victor's behaviour continues to worry his father.
- A letter from Elizabeth hastens Victor's return to Geneva.
- Elizabeth and Victor marry and go to Italy by boat for their honeymoon, stopping in Evian for their wedding night.

WHY IS THIS CHAPTER IMPORTANT?

A Victor is certain it is his own life that is at risk as the wedding night approaches.

B Victor **marries** Elizabeth and the couple begin their honeymoon.

KEY CONTEXT (A03)

Evian, famous for its mineral water, was a fashionable spa resort on the southern shores of Lake Geneva.

TOP TIP (A01)

Notice how Shelley uses Elizabeth's letter to speed up the marriage subplot and, in turn, the oncoming conflict promised by the monster.

AIMING HIGH: ANALYSING FORM

The very best answers will comment on Shelley's use of form. While not an epistolary novel (written only in the form of letters), *Frankenstein* includes letters by some characters and begins and ends with Walton's letters to his sister. Letters are one of the ways in which a variety of characters' perspectives are shown and through which readers gain valuable insights into the characters. Elizabeth's letter in this chapter has much in common with the letter in Chapter VI: it is affectionate but concerned. She affirms her love for her childhood sweetheart but is anxious to know whether he is in love with another woman. The letter reminds Victor of the monster's threat, *'I will be with you on your wedding-night'* (p. 192), but in his reply he reveals only that he has a 'dreadful' secret (p. 193) that he will reveal to her on the day after their marriage. What do you feel Shelley's use of letters adds to the novel?

KEY QUOTATION: PAST AND PRESENT (A01)

Elizabeth's letter reminds the reader of the happy childhood she and Victor shared. Victor's response – which he reads and re-reads – shows that it briefly rekindles this innocent happiness: 'softened feelings stole into my heart, and dared to whisper paradisiacal dreams of love and joy; but the apple was already eaten' (p. 193). Victor's comment that 'the apple was already eaten' dramatically punctures this brief dream of happiness. The contrast between 'paradisiacal dreams' and the eaten apple is a direct allusion to the Bible story of Adam and Eve, who are banished from paradise for tasting the forbidden fruit. Shelley is establishing a tragic contrast between the past and the present, between Victor's life before and after his discovery.

VOLUME THREE, CHAPTER VI: TWO DEATHS

SUMMARY

- On their wedding night, Victor paces the house to ensure that his bride is safe.
- Suddenly, Victor hears Elizabeth scream from the bedroom. He finds her dead with black fingermarks on her neck. She has been murdered by the monster in his absence.
- Victor sees the monster grinning at the window and shoots at him.
- He assembles a party of people from the inn to pursue the monster but they fail to find him.
- Victor returns to Geneva with the miserable news. The misfortune is too much for Alphonse, who dies.
- Victor tells a magistrate the whole story of the monster's foul deeds, hoping the law will hunt him down. The magistrate promises to punish the monster should he ever be found, but is incredulous about Victor's testimony.
- Victor swears to destroy his creation, devoting himself 'either in my life or death, to his destruction' (p. 204).

WHY IS THIS CHAPTER IMPORTANT?

A   Elizabeth is **murdered** by the monster on her wedding night.
B   Alphonse dies on hearing the news, leaving Victor as **solitary** a figure as the monster himself.
C   Victor vows to **destroy** the monster.

TOP TIP: WRITING ABOUT SETTING (A03)

It is important that you can comment on the writer's choice of setting. In setting the scene for Victor and Elizabeth's wedding night in Evian, Shelley first describes a pleasant scene 'of waters, woods, and mountains' (p. 198), only then to introduce more sinister details. Shelley describes the moon appearing – a motif frequently associated with the monster's imminent appearance – and the wind rising 'with great violence' (p. 198). The gathering darkness, the violence of the rainstorm and Victor's growing nervousness create tension. Part of the horror derives from the fact that Victor is away from his bride checking the inn for safety when she is murdered. Just as he begins to hope that something had prevented the monster 'executing his menaces' (p. 199), Victor is alerted by the terrifying scream, the stuff of nightmares.

KEY CONTEXT (A03)

The murder of the bride by the monster in the bridal suite is the central episode on which so many horror films are based. *The Bride of Frankenstein* is one of nearly sixty films that use the Frankenstein story.

TOP TIP (A02)

The literary term for when inanimate objects or nature reflect or mirror human behaviour and feelings is pathetic fallacy. Shelley uses this, for example, on p. 198 when Victor says that the moon 'dimmed her rays' and the waves were 'restless'.

CHECKPOINT 20 (A01)

What reasons does the magistrate give to explain why the monster will be hard to track down?

VOLUME THREE, CHAPTER VII: THE PURSUIT OF THE MONSTER

SUMMARY

- Victor goes to the graveyard and calls on the spirits of the dead to help him in his revenge. He hears the monster laugh.
- Victor begins his pursuit of the monster across Europe and Russia. As the chase leads him to the north, the monster taunts him sporadically.
- Eventually, just as Victor 'appeared almost within grasp of [his] foe' (p. 211), the ice cracks and he is left drifting.
- Victor is saved by Walton, who listens to his astonishing story and laments his declining health.
- In letters to his sister, Walton describes Victor's death.
- The monster makes his final appearance and tells Walton that he will 'consume to ashes this miserable frame' (p. 224) before climbing out of the window and disappearing.

WHY IS THIS CHAPTER IMPORTANT?

A Victor's sighting of the ship brings us back to the start of the book from a new **perspective**.

B Victor's request that Walton should destroy the creature is crucial to setting up the final **climax** of the novel.

C Victor dies and the monster tells Walton he too will die – by committing **suicide**.

KEY CONTEXT (A03)

The Romantic writers were very enthusiastic readers of early travel books and were inspired by them. Shelley herself travelled widely and was familiar with many of the places she describes in *Frankenstein*.

TOP TIP (A01)

Consider how Shelley writes about the self-destructive power of vengeful feelings in this chapter, for example: 'I was cursed by some devil, and carried about with me my eternal hell' (p. 207).

KEY CHARACTERS: VICTOR AND THE MONSTER **A01**

As the novel reaches its climax, there is a confusion of roles: it is difficult to decide which character has the upper hand and who is pursuing whom. Victor pursues the monster in a sledge, but the monster taunts Victor in the graveyard and leaves him food to keep him alive.

The monster's actions clearly suggest that he wants Victor to experience, and suffer, the same fate as him. The two characters seem to merge: they are both isolated and hate each other, but are also fatally linked.

KEY SETTING: THE PURSUIT **A01**

The setting becomes global as Victor hunts down the monster. The quest becomes epic; as Victor says, his 'wanderings began which are to cease but with life' (p. 205). He resolves to kill the monster or die in the attempt and is prepared to chase him across the world. The trail takes him from the 'blue Mediterranean' to the 'wilds of Tartary and Russia' (p. 207). Victor pursues the monster for months over land and sea. The monster taunts Victor by leaving signs and messages. Finally, he turns northwards and follows the route taken by Walton.

Victor hires a sledge and dogs to chase his enemy. He almost catches the monster and utters 'a wild cry of ecstasy' (pp. 210–11) when he sees the 'dark speck upon the dusky plain' (p. 210), but they are separated when the ice splits. Victor is sinking when he sees Walton's ship, a scene which carries echoes of Victor's earlier thoughts of death (Volume Three, Chapter III): 'I looked upon the sea, it was to be my grave' (p. 176). But Victor is saved by Walton and his crew, and ends his narrative by pleading with Walton to kill the monster if he ever sees him, 'for my task is still unfulfilled' (p. 212).

KEY FORM: WALTON AS NARRATOR **A02**

Walton resumes his narration in the form of letters to his sister and we re-join the story where we started. We are reminded that Victor has been telling his story to Walton. This is an effective technique for creating immediacy and directness; Shelley seems to want her readers to feel they are in Walton's shoes.

Shelley's choice of form also helps make the unbelievable seem believable. Walton has seen 'the letters of Felix and Safie' (p. 213) and glimpsed 'the apparition of the monster seen from our ship' (p. 213). Within the imagined world of the novel, this is proof of Victor's story, contrasting with the magistrate's incredulity at the end of the previous chapter.

Walton's final letters bring the story back to the present and to the question of what will become of both Victor and his creation. Walton presents the character of Victor in a more dignified light than Victor portrays himself. In Walton's eyes, Victor is a tragic hero: a great man who has become a wreck and who knows 'the greatness of his fall' (p. 214).

KEY CONTEXT **A03**

The 'Double' is a common idea in Gothic literature. It suggests that a person contains two separate but connected selves. Usually one of the selves is rational and the other is irrational and often violent. Robert Louis Stevenson's short novel, *The Strange Case of Dr Jekyll and Mr Hyde* (1886), explores this idea as Jekyll drinks a potion that unleashes his evil double, Hyde. We can see the same idea in *Frankenstein* as Shelley blurs the lines between Victor Frankenstein and the monster he creates.

KEY CONTEXT **A03**

Mary Shelley's mother had originally been involved with a Captain Gilbert Imlay, an American, who had made many expeditions into the wilder parts of America.

TOP TIP **A01**

Despite his moral tale on the dangers of knowledge and ambition, Victor still feels the need to be 'engaged in any high undertaking' (p. 215).

TOP TIP A02

Look carefully at how Walton – who is mourning the loss of his friend and mindful of Victor's dying wish – reacts to the sight of the monster, and at what he says to him.

KEY THEME: AMBITION A01

Surrounded by glaciers and faced with the prospect of sinking, Walton realises that he has endangered the lives of his crew and that his ambitious 'mad schemes are the cause' (p. 215). Walton's youthful ambition and taste for adventure in earlier letters contrasts with his current 'dread' of 'a mutiny caused by … despair' (p. 216). Walton's reaction to his crew's threat of mutiny mirrors Victor's initial response to the creature: Walton cannot 'in justice … refuse' this demand (p. 216). Victor, however, gives a rousing speech, urging them to continue their great enterprise. It is ironic that Victor seems ignorant of the moral of his own tale when he makes this elevated speech as, a few pages later, he is urging Walton to learn from his example and 'avoid ambition' (p. 220).

EXAM FOCUS: COMMENTING ON CHARACTER AND LANGUAGE A02

You may be asked to analyse the language of key characters. Read this example by one student, commenting on the monster's language when he meets Walton:

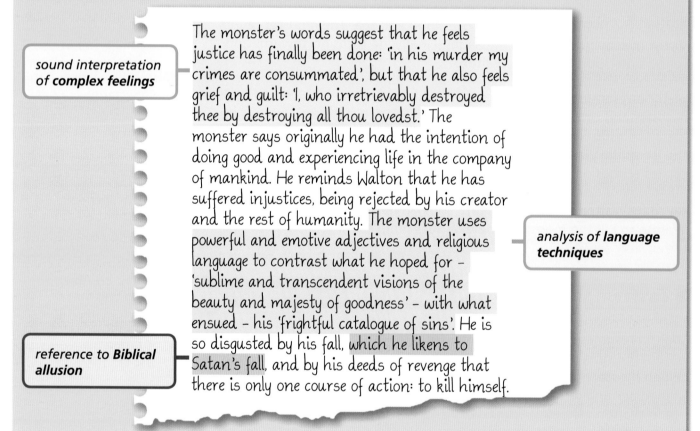

sound interpretation of **complex feelings**

The monster's words suggest that he feels justice has finally been done: 'in his murder my crimes are consummated', but that he also feels grief and guilt: 'I, who irretrievably destroyed thee by destroying all thou lovedst.' The monster says originally he had the intention of doing good and experiencing life in the company of mankind. He reminds Walton that he has suffered injustices, being rejected by his creator and the rest of humanity. The monster uses powerful and emotive adjectives and religious language to contrast what he hoped for – 'sublime and transcendent visions of the beauty and majesty of goodness' – with what ensued – his 'frightful catalogue of sins'. He is so disgusted by his fall, which he likens to Satan's fall, and by his deeds of revenge that there is only one course of action: to kill himself.

analysis of **language techniques**

reference to **Biblical allusion**

Now you try it:

This paragraph needs a final sentence to draw everything together. Add a sentence that explores the meaning and effect of the monster's language in this passage. Start: '*In this passage, …*'

TOP TIP: WRITING ABOUT THE FINAL SPEECH A01

Note how the monster's final speech sums up the tragedy and themes of the book. It shows the contrast between his early kindness and his evil revenge.

PROGRESS AND REVISION CHECK

SECTION ONE: CHECK YOUR KNOWLEDGE

Answer these quick questions to test your basic knowledge of the novel, its characters and events:

1. How is Margaret Saville related to Captain Walton?
2. In which country is Geneva?
3. Name Victor's mother, father and brothers.
4. What is the name of the university Victor attends?
5. What does Victor study there?
6. How tall is the monster?
7. Why does Victor make him that size?
8. Which distinctive marks does the monster leave on the bodies of his victims?
9. Why does Justine Moritz confess to William's murder?
10. What do the villagers attack the monster with in Volume Two, Chapter III?
11. What instrument does old De Lacey play?
12. How does the monster secretly help the De Lacey family?
13. What does the monster refer to as 'a godlike science' in Volume Two, Chapter IV?
14. Who escapes from where with the help of Felix? Where do they escape to?
15. What is the name of the epic poem by John Milton that reminds the monster of his own situation?
16. Who is Mr Kirwin and why is Victor brought before him?
17. How does Victor misinterpret the monster's threat about his wedding night?
18. Where do the Frankensteins plan to spend their honeymoon and why do they stop en route?
19. How does the monster say he will die?
20. Which mythological figure brought fire to mankind and why is he significant in *Frankenstein*?

SECTION TWO: CHECK YOUR UNDERSTANDING

Here are two tasks about the significance of particular moments in the novel. These require more thought and slightly longer responses. In each case, try to write at least three to four paragraphs.

Task 1: Look again at Shelley's account of Justine's trial and imprisonment in Volume One, Chapter VIII. What is significant about this account? Think about:

- The importance of Justine as a character
- The response of other characters to her situation

Task 2: In Volume Two, Chapters I and II, why is the section in which Victor walks in the Alpine valleys important? Think about:

- What the Alpine scenery represents for Victor and its effect on his mood
- The way the monster suddenly appears

PROGRESS CHECK

GOOD PROGRESS

I can:

- understand how Shelley has sequenced and revealed events.   ☐
- refer to the importance of key events in the novel.   ☐
- select well-chosen evidence, including key quotations, to support my ideas.   ☐

EXCELLENT PROGRESS

I can:

- refer in depth to main and minor events and how they contribute to the development of the plot.   ☐
- understand how Shelley has carefully ordered or revealed events for particular effects.   ☐
- draw on a range of carefully selected key evidence, including quotations, to support my ideas.   ☐

WHO'S WHO?

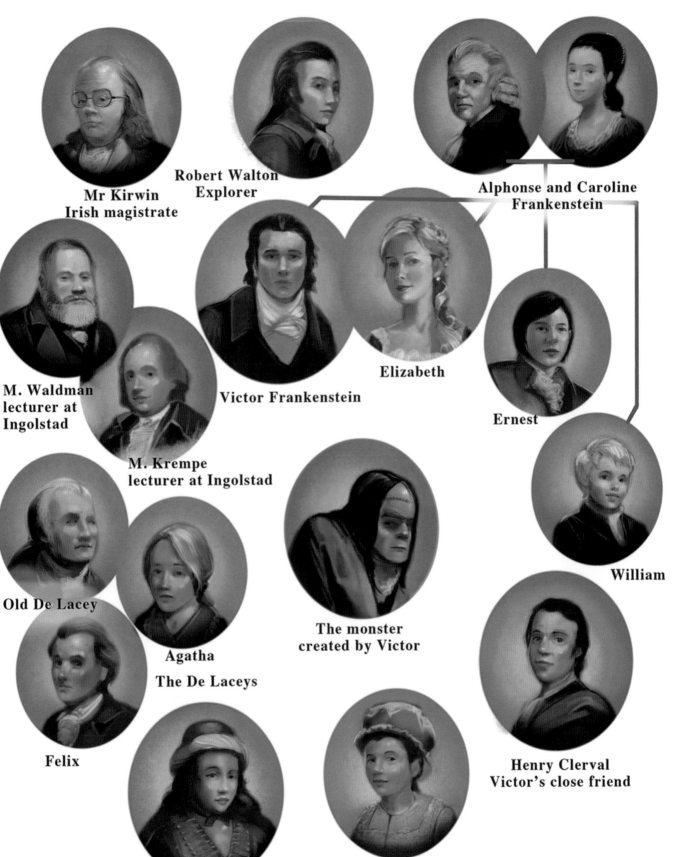

Mr Kirwin
Irish magistrate

Robert Walton
Explorer

Alphonse and Caroline
Frankenstein

M. Waldman
lecturer at
Ingolstad

M. Krempe
lecturer at Ingolstad

Victor Frankenstein

Elizabeth

Ernest

William

Old De Lacey

Agatha

The De Laceys

The monster
created by Victor

Henry Clerval
Victor's close friend

Felix

Justine Moritz
the Frankensteins' maid

Safie
Turkish merchant's daughter,
friend of the De Laceys

ROBERT WALTON

WALTON'S ROLE IN THE NOVEL

Walton is an ambitious man, an explorer of twenty-eight who writes a series of letters to his sister, Margaret, about his journey towards the North Pole. During the novel:

- He is depicted as a Romantic man whose imagination and sense of adventure lead him into danger.
- He saves Victor and hears his story.
- He likes and admires Victor immediately and begins to 'love him as a brother' (p. 28).
- His need to succeed on his voyage blinds him to his crew's threat of mutiny.
- He sees the monster for himself and speaks to him at the very end of the novel.

WALTON'S IMPORTANCE TO THE NOVEL AS A WHOLE

Walton is the narrator who begins the novel and his concerns set up the main themes and issues. Not only does Walton begin and end the main tale, but Victor Frankenstein is first seen through his eyes and Walton is Victor's audience as his own story unfolds. Shelley draws several important parallels between Walton and Victor.

TOP TIP (A02)

There is little physical description of Walton. This means you will need to focus on his emotional qualities, mental characteristics and the way he tells his story – his voice.

EXAM FOCUS: WRITING ABOUT WALTON

A01

Key point	Evidence / Further meaning
● Walton is emotionally volatile and unpredictable, a man who is often at the mercy of his feelings rather than being in control of them.	● He describes his emotions as he departs on his expedition as a 'trembling sensation, half pleasurable and half fearful' (p. 21). ● He finishes one letter to his sister 'My swelling heart involuntarily pours itself out thus' (p. 24).
● Poems, books and childish fantasies first inspired his desire for exploration.	● In his early years, he read accounts of seafaring voyages and poetry (p. 16). ● He also wrote poetry and dreamed of becoming a famous poet (p. 16).
● His letters tend to alternate between hope and gloom.	● At the beginning of the novel, he writes passionately and joyfully about how he imagines the North Pole (p. 15). ● This contrasts with his claim that his 'spirits are often depressed' (p. 17).
● He is a determined character.	● He tells his sister that his 'resolutions' are 'as fixed as fate' (p. 21). ● At the end of the novel, he says that 'I had rather die than return shamefully' (p. 218), though eventually he has to relent and agrees to return home.

TOP TIP: COMPARING WALTON AND VICTOR

A01

You should consider how Shelley draws parallels between Walton and Victor throughout the novel; the two characters resemble each other in their loneliness and desire for friendship, their curiosity and self-education and the force of their ambition. Walton's prayers for a friend to regulate his mind seem to be answered in Victor, who is worried that Walton is pursuing the same course as he did in the past: Victor does not want Walton's desire for knowledge to be a 'serpent to sting' him (p. 31). Walton, therefore, appears to be presented with an image of his potential future self: a man wrecked and destroyed by his own ambition.

Both characters fail to realise the effect their actions can have on others. Walton's resistance to the idea of turning back for home mirrors the relationship between Victor and the monster. The crew becomes the rebellious monster of Walton's creation that stands up for its own rights. It is ironic that both Walton and Victor feel themselves to be victims, yet both seem at least partially aware that their own 'mad schemes' (p. 215) are also to blame for their misfortunes.

KEY CONTEXT

A03

Walton hopes to discover 'a passage near the pole to those countries, to reach which at present so many months are requisite' (p. 16). Such a route had been sought by explorers for centuries and Shelley seems to be suggesting here that the young and inexperienced Walton has set himself an unrealistic goal. The Northwest Passage was finally navigated by the Norwegian explorer Roald Amundsen between 1903 and 1906.

VICTOR FRANKENSTEIN

VICTOR'S ROLE IN THE NOVEL

Victor is the eldest son in a respectable Genevan family. During the novel:

- He reminisces about his happy childhood.
- He becomes increasingly interested in science and attends Ingolstadt University.
- His enthusiasm about discovering the magnificent secrets of life leads him to tamper with graveyards and dead bodies and eventually to create a new life – the monster.
- His life becomes more and more unbearable as the monster commits appalling acts against Victor's loved ones.
- He pursues the monster to the North Pole.
- He finds an understanding friend in Walton to whom he narrates his life story shortly before he dies.

VICTOR'S IMPORTANCE TO THE NOVEL AS A WHOLE

Victor is the second of three narrators, and the central character of the novel that bears his name. *Frankenstein* tells the story of Victor's obsessive pursuit of knowledge and its consequences. Shelley shows us throughout the novel how the destinies of Victor and his creation are irreversibly intertwined.

TOP TIP (A02)

Collect quotations that illustrate the emotional tension in Victor and make a note of the effect on the reader of each one.

TOP TIP (A02)

Consider how Shelley's choice of the name 'Victor' for her protagonist becomes increasingly ironic as the novel progresses. By the end of the novel, Victor and the monster resemble each other in many ways and share a similar tragic fate.

EXAM FOCUS: WRITING ABOUT VICTOR

Key point	Evidence / Further meaning
• We see early on that the combination of his 'thirst for knowledge' and his 'child's blindness' will be dangerous (p. 42).	• In Chapter IV, he is taken over by his work: he forgets his family and does not consider what he will do with his creation once it is brought to life. • However, the writing is so powerful that the reader is carried along with Victor on his exciting journey and we also become 'exalted' (p. 54).
• Victor can seem either partially aware of his faults or unable to admit to them.	• His own ambition and passion for 'glory' (p. 42) are his worst enemies and he brings devastation upon himself. • Victor increasingly contradicts himself as his problems deepen. Divided between feelings of guilt and revenge, he alternately blames himself and the monster for the deaths of William and Justine.
• Having worked so tirelessly to create new life, Victor's feelings towards his creation are of fear and disgust and he neglects the monster.	• Victor appears to feel little remorse for abandoning the monster. Shelley suggests that Victor's duty towards his family and humanity would have been better served by doing his duty to the monster (Volume Two, Chapter IX and Volume Three, Chapter III). • However, our sympathy for the monster may lead us to underestimate the foulness of William's murder. It is understandable that Victor continues to see the monster as a 'devil' (p. 173).
• Victor becomes increasingly self-absorbed.	• Victor's knowledge of the monster isolates him from his friends and family. • He tries to protect his loved ones but makes fatal errors, such as misinterpreting the monster's warning 'I shall be with you on your wedding-night' (p. 173).

AIMING HIGH: CHARACTER AND VIEWPOINT

Victor is loved by almost everyone: his family, Clerval, M. Krempe and M. Waldman, and even Mr Kirwin admires him. Walton introduces him as a 'celestial spirit', a 'divine wanderer' with a 'never-failing power of judgment' (p. 30). Yet these images only tell half the story. Does Shelley seek to show the reader that despite everything Victor is still a good man, or do these ironies simply reveal the short-sightedness of her other characters?

The reader often feels ambivalent towards Victor. Like most tragic heroes, the personality traits that make him a powerful character are the same ones that lead to his ruin. To what extent do you find Victor sympathetic?

TOP TIP **A02**

Consider the significance of some of the names Shelley gives to her characters, such as 'Elizabeth', 'Clerval' and 'Justine'. For example, the name 'Victor' means winner.

ALPHONSE

ALPHONSE'S ROLE IN THE NOVEL

Alphonse Frankenstein, Victor's father, is depicted as a kind, gentle and respectable man of wealth. During the novel:

- The reader learns how he found a secure home for the orphaned Caroline Beaufort, whom he eventually married.
- Their first-born son, Victor, is sent to university in Ingolstadt.
- He very much wants Victor and Elizabeth to marry.
- He comes to his son's aid when Victor is suspected of murdering Clerval and imprisoned.
- He dies shortly after Elizabeth's death.

EXAM FOCUS: WRITING ABOUT ALPHONSE   **A01**

Key point	Evidence / Further meaning
• Alphonse was loyal to his friend Beaufort.	• Alphonse was determined to seek out his needy friend. • He was willing to give Beaufort money and assistance.
• Victor views Alphonse as a good father.	• Victor believes Alphonse fulfilled his responsibilities as a parent with an 'active spirit of tenderness' (p. 35).
• Alphonse can also be distant and formal.	• Alphonse does not take the time to explain to Victor why he is dismissive about what Victor has been reading.

TOP TIP   **A02**

Victor's earliest memories of his father's 'smile of benevolent pleasure' (p. 35) do not give a full picture of Alphonse, who uses a reproachful tone in his letters and can be distant and formal.

TOP TIP: ALPHONSE AS A PARENT   **A01**

Consider the different ways in which Alphonse supports and guides his son, and the personal qualities he brings to his role as parent throughout the various stages of his son's life: as a child, during his university studies, and as an adult. Compare him with the other fathers and 'father figures' the reader encounters in the course of the book: Clerval's merchant father, old De Lacey, Caroline's father Beaufort, and also Victor who is a kind of parent figure to the monster.

ELIZABETH

ELIZABETH'S ROLE IN THE NOVEL

Elizabeth is Alphonse and Caroline's adored adopted daughter, a caring and loyal figure in Victor's life. During the novel:

- She supports and cares for Victor and grows anxious about Victor's welfare when he becomes withdrawn and troubled.
- She believes in Justine's innocence and is prepared to say so in court.
- She becomes like a mother to Victor's young brothers and is grief-stricken by William's death.
- She marries Victor and is murdered by the monster on the couple's wedding-night.

EXAM FOCUS: WRITING ABOUT ELIZABETH **A01**

Key point	Evidence / Further meaning
• Elizabeth is introduced from the beginning as a model character whose inner qualities are matched by her physical beauty.	• Victor describes 'her smile, her soft voice, the sweet glance of her celestial eyes' (p. 39).
• Elizabeth creates strong and loyal relationships.	• Victor introduces Elizabeth as a 'beautiful and adored companion' (p. 37). • She becomes like a mother to Victor's younger brothers and writes tenderly about them (Chapter VI).
• She shows kindness and gives help to others.	• She is able to 'soften' Clerval's ambitions and 'subdue' Victor's violent temper (p. 40). • She courageously defends Justine in court with a 'simple and powerful appeal' (p. 86).

TOP TIP: ELIZABETH'S VIEWS AND IDEALS **A01**

Make sure you consider the views and ideals espoused by Elizabeth in the course of the novel. Elizabeth is a forward-thinking woman who has democratic values. She is proud of being Genevan and is happy to see equality between the classes in Switzerland, 'our fortunate country' (p. 66). However, she is also naive and idealistic. Her belief in human goodness is shattered by Justine's unjust execution. She realises that 'vice' is not 'imaginary' but real (p. 95).

TOP TIP **A01**

Remind yourself of what we know about Elizabeth's biological parents and what we learn about the circumstances of her adoption.

THE MONSTER

THE MONSTER'S ROLE IN THE NOVEL

The monster is a gigantic eight-foot-tall creature made by Victor from the parts of dead bodies. During the novel:

- He is created by Victor, who is terrified of him.
- He is attacked by villagers because of how he looks.
- He finds a shelter near a poor family and observes them lead their lives.
- He learns about human society and learns language.
- He wants to befriend the De Laceys, but terrifies them and flees.
- He kills William and implicates Justine in the murder.
- His wish that Victor create a companion for him is ultimately refused.
- He kills Clerval and, later, Elizabeth.
- He is pursued by Victor to the North Pole.
- After Victor's death, the monster mourns him and says he too will die.

THE MONSTER'S IMPORTANCE TO THE NOVEL AS A WHOLE

The monster is Victor's creation; a hideous creature who inspires fear and causes bloodshed and anguish but who also wins the reader's sympathy. His impossible predicament is seen as the direct consequence of Victor's soaring ambition. The lives and destinies of Victor and the monster, protagonist and antagonist, are interconnected throughout the novel – with tragic consequences for them both.

TOP TIP (A02)

Look again at where the monster is described (Volume One, Chapter V; Volume Two, Chapters II, IV and IX; Volume Three, Chapters III and VII) and summarise what we learn about his physical appearance.

EXAM FOCUS: WRITING ABOUT THE MONSTER (A01)

Key point	Evidence / Further meaning
● Events make the reader pity the monster.	● The brutal attacks on him by the villagers, Felix and the peasant who shoots him, make us pity him. ● He experiences 'despondence and mortification' (p. 117) on seeing his own reflection in a pool.
● The monster is a victim of prejudice	● The barrier between him and humanity is his physical ugliness, nothing more. ● Even when attempting to help or seek protection from others, his intentions are misinterpreted. ● The monster hopes that a blind man and a young child will be free of prejudice, but they are not.
● The way he is mistreated and rejected by human beings turns him from a creature into a monster.	● He begins to see himself as 'a monster, a blot upon the earth' (p. 123). ● His demand for a companion is his last hope and a justice that Victor finally denies.

AIMING HIGH: INTERPRETING CHARACTERS

The monster's unnatural creation, ugliness and power are reflected in Victor's first descriptions of him as a 'demoniacal corpse' (p. 59). Victor portrays him as otherworldly when he sees him in the Alps coming towards him with 'superhuman speed' (p.101). The monster's strength is seen in his physical endurance (Volume Three, Chapter VII). Shelley's use of satanic imagery to depict his emotions reveals him to be an evil character who should be feared.

However, it could also be said that this imaginative and sensitive wanderer is essentially a Romantic hero. His hope for a female is denied him because of his killing of William and his framing of Justine, acts he later regrets. His final speeches are elevated and noble and the vision he has of his own suicide is exalted and sublime (Volume Three, Chapter VII).

The reader sees – particularly in the sections the monster narrates – that his fury and misery are the consequences of his loneliness and rejection. He begins life as an innocent and harmless being with a natural attraction to the wonders of nature and to the human race. He is a creature of good deeds: he collects wood for the De Laceys, saves a girl from drowning and is a vegetarian. In the monster, Shelley has created a complex character: a nameless ugly creature, a victim of prejudice who wins our sympathy, and a despairing outcast who becomes envious, vengeful and murderous. It is important that you can see all sides of the character and come to your own personal interpretation of Shelley's monster. How do you view the monster?

TOP TIP (A03)

Keep track of the monster's education – from the natural world, from people and from literature. Ask yourself the following questions: What does the monster learn? How does he feel about what he has learned? How does the monster begin to view himself?

HENRY CLERVAL

Henry Clerval is a dear friend of Victor's. Throughout the novel, Shelley presents Clerval as a supportive, loyal and benign figure in Victor's life. He serves various literary purposes:

- Along with Victor and Walton, Clerval is presented as an adventurous and spirited young man: 'a boy of singular talent and fancy' (p. 39). His father, a merchant, wants him to pursue a career in commerce rather than a 'liberal education' (p. 46) but eventually relents to his son's wishes, and Clerval becomes Victor's fellow student.

- He is one of several characters to whom Victor is very close but to whom he cannot tell the truth about what torments him. This adds to the sense of Victor's isolation and to an atmosphere of suspense about what tragic events might await Victor and his virtuous and trusting friends.

- His sensitivity to nature is praised by Victor; what 'others regard only with admiration, he loved with ardour' (p. 161). Clerval's joy and 'enthusiastic imagination' (p. 161) only deepen Victor's gloom and serve to remind us of the growing contrast between the two characters.

- His death in Volume Three is another devastating loss for an increasingly desperate and isolated Victor, who is accused of his murder.

TOP TIP (A01)

Notice Shelley's use of dramatic irony when Victor adopts a mournful tone as he praises his dear friend Henry Clerval in Volume Three, Chapter I. The reader begins to fear that Clerval's enthusiasm and joy are to be short lived.

WILLIAM FRANKENSTEIN

Although a minor character, William has a huge impact on the story. He is the youngest son of Alphonse, a beautiful young boy 'with sweet laughing blue eyes … and curling hair' (p. 68). He is murdered by the monster because he refuses to be his friend and reveals his family's name. His death serves several literary purposes:

- It is revealed to Victor in a letter and the reader is as shocked as Victor that the boy who was 'rosy with health' (p. 68) is dead. The tragic news forces Victor to return home and encounter the monster on the way. His suspicion that the creature is the murderer raises expectations in the reader.

- It makes us sympathise with Victor. After overcoming the shock of having created a grotesque, living monster, this second misfortune follows quickly. His return to normal health is short-lived.

- It forms the basis of the subplot involving Justine. This allows Shelley to introduce political themes that are central to the relationship between Victor and the monster.

- It makes Victor mistrust the monster. This mistrust makes him destroy the female creature.

- The death is written about for a second time when the monster gives his own version of events. We see that the monster is naive in believing that William will be 'unprejudiced' (p. 144) because he is a child.

- It introduces the theme of mutual revenge between Victor and the monster.

DE LACEY

De Lacey is a blind old man who is kind and gentle. The monster, who observes the De Lacey family closely, describes his 'expression of goodness that bestowed pleasure even upon me' (p. 115) and hopes to befriend him. The monster also learns that De Lacey was 'descended from a good family in France' and had lived 'in affluence' (p. 125). He serves many literary purposes:

- His warm-hearted goodness to his family attract the monster, who pins all his hopes of happiness on befriending him.
- Although his son's actions have brought him into poverty and exile, he doesn't love Felix any less. His forgiving nature appeals to the monster.
- The strong family relationships he has created emphasise the monster's loneliness.
- He is the only character who shows the monster any kindness. His blindness prevents him from being prejudiced.
- The monster's desperation scares De Lacey and makes Felix misinterpret the monster's intentions.

MINOR CHARACTERS

Minor characters enable the author to:

- move the plot forward
- develop a theme
- help us to learn more about the major characters.

The novel is populated with a great number of minor characters used by Shelley to mirror a quality of one or more of the major characters. By drawing these parallels, Shelley prompts the reader to compare and contrast the characters more closely. The minor characters can be grouped together in the following ways.

VIRTUOUS WOMEN

Shelley's female characters mostly represent kindness, courage and compassion. **Caroline Beaufort's** kindness towards the poor is a 'passion' rather than a 'duty' (p. 36) because she remembers being poor herself. Her adoption of **Elizabeth**, who embodies many of the same qualities, recalls her own history.

Justine Moritz, neglected by her mother, helps and is helped by the Frankenstein family and becomes a trusted companion. When she is tried for William's murder, she is seen to possess extraordinary moral courage, and her innocence is not in doubt for Elizabeth, Victor or the reader. She describes herself as 'resigned to the fate awaiting me' (p. 89) and her Christian faith remains strong.

De Lacey's 'ever-gentle' daughter **Agatha** (p. 120) and Safie, the 'always gay and happy' daughter of the Turkish merchant (p. 121), also demonstrate kindness towards others and bear their adverse circumstances admirably, showing strength of character.

KEY CONTEXT (A03)

Mary Shelley's mother, Mary Wollstonecraft, wrote a book called *A Vindication of the Rights of Woman* (1792). She believed in women's education and argued that women's work as mothers and as companions to their husbands should have more status. Percy Bysshe Shelley wrote in the Preface to *Frankenstein* that 'the amiableness of domestic affection' was an important theme in his wife's novel.

KEY CONTEXT (A03)

Hugh Walpole called Mary Shelley's father William Godwin, 'one of the greatest monsters exhibited by history'. Walpole and other critics believed that Godwin's radical and utopian ideas about the human race would lead to destruction and anarchy.

INADEQUATE FATHERS

There are many fathers who fail in their parental role. The **fathers of Clerval**, **Walton** and **Safie** try to stop their children from pursuing their own interests. Their behaviour recalls **Alphonse's** dismissal of Victor's book. The Turk's tyrannical behaviour also mirrors Victor's attitude to the monster.

Furthermore, **Elizabeth's father** abandons her, and **Caroline's father** makes his daughter suffer by hiding from society after he lost his fortune. Victor, as the monster's creator, fails to show any parental feelings towards him, leaving him isolated and lonely. All these fathers contrast with **De Lacey's** qualities as a parent.

AMBITIOUS SONS

Victor, **Felix**, **Clerval** and **Walton** all have passionate ambitions to be benefactors to mankind in some way. Despite their merits, Felix's plans cause suffering to his family and Walton's plans have the potential to be fatal. While women appear to be preserving and creating human relationships, men seem to destroy them. The stories of the more minor characters mirror Victor's dangerous but well-meaning ambitions.

SCIENTISTS

We encounter three scientists other than Victor. The first is **Alphonse's friend** – 'a man of great research in natural philosophy' (p. 42) who explains electricity and galvanism. These become central ideas to Victor's work. **M. Waldman** also has a huge influence on Victor because he explains the miracles of modern science. The other lecturer, **M. Krempe**, recalls Alphonse by his sarcastic dismissal of Victor's passion for alchemy.

JUDGES

The only professional characters other than scientists are judges. This highlights the theme of people judging each other and the reader judging the characters. Although judges are responsible for the wellbeing of others, only **Mr Kirwin** decides to seek actively for the real truth.

CROWDS

There are three crowds of people: those **at Justine's trial**, the **Irish crowd** who accuse Victor of murder, and the **villagers** who attack the monster. All are brutal, short sighted and dangerous.

REVISION FOCUS: LEARN KEY QUOTATIONS

It is vital to support all your points about *Frankenstein* with quotations. You will need to be ready to write about any of the characters that appear in the novel. Short quotations that you can embed within a sentence are of particular use when you are writing in timed conditions. Challenge yourself to select quotations of no more than eight words about each character and record them in a separate document for each character. Look back at them often and aim to learn them by heart.

PROGRESS AND REVISION CHECK

SECTION ONE: CHECK YOUR KNOWLEDGE

1. Which character is the daughter of a Milanese nobleman but was brought up by a peasant family?

2. Which character is the son of a Genevan merchant and a loyal friend to Victor?

3. Who are Krempe and Waldman?

4. 'The silver hair and benevolent countenance of the aged cottager won my reverence.' Who is the monster describing here?

5. Who does Victor refer to as 'daemon', 'fiend' and 'the being'?

6. Who fell into poverty and was looked after by his daughter until his death?

7. Who describes his 'self-educated' status as an 'evil'?

8. Who prefers the open air, hill-climbing and rowing to study?

9. How is Safie described when she approaches the De Lacey's cottage?

10. 'my companion, my sister...!' To whom is Elizabeth speaking?

TOP TIP (A01)

Answer these quick questions to test your basic knowledge of the novel's characters.

SECTION TWO: CHECK YOUR UNDERSTANDING.

Task: How does Shelley convey Victor's ambitious nature:

- in his own narrative, and
- in the sections narrated by Walton?

TOP TIP (A01)

This task requires more thought and a slightly longer response. Try to write at least three to four paragraphs.

PROGRESS CHECK

GOOD PROGRESS

I can:

- explain the significance of the main characters in how the action develops. ☐
- refer to how they are described by Shelley and how this affects the way we see them. ☐

EXCELLENT PROGRESS

I can:

- analyse in detail how Shelley has shaped and developed characters over the course of the novel. ☐
- infer key ideas, themes and issues from the ways characters and relationships are presented by Shelley. ☐

THEME TRACKER (A01)

The meaning of the monster

- Vol. One, Ch. V, p. 59: Victor refers to his creation as a 'miserable monster'.

- Vol. Two, Ch. V, p. 123: The monster questions his origins and identity.

- Vol. Two, Ch. IX, p. 148: Victor is 'moved' by the monster's situation.

THEMES

THE MEANING OF THE MONSTER

At the heart of *Frankenstein* are the monster's questions, 'Who was I? What was I?' (p. 131). The answers remain an enticing mystery. Readers have put forward a wide range of views and interpretations.

The novel has been seen as:

- A moral tale or fable about the conflict between good and evil, or a warning about the dangers of scientific progress

- A Romantic tale exploring the tragic ruin of two heroes. Victor and the monster become powerful symbols of loneliness, destroyed by their own talents and needs

- A psychological tale about unnatural desires and dangerous ambitions

- A social tale about a parent–child relationship, showing the sad consequences of a father failing to perform his duties

- A political tale in which the monster symbolises people who have been denied their rights of freedom, equality and fraternity. Victor stands for a tyrannical ruler

- A philosophical tale asking, 'What is the origin of evil? Does it arise from our nature or does it come from the world around us – from society?' Initially the creature is good, but becomes a monster by the cruel ways human beings treat him

TOP TIP (A01)

Keep track of instances when Shelley seems to be portraying humans – in their ugly and violent reaction to the unknown and the different – as more monstrous than the monster.

TOP TIP: DEVELOP YOUR OWN INTERPRETATION (A01)

The best way to develop your own interpretation is to study the themes of the book, such as knowledge, ambition, prejudice and justice, and how they are developed, by looking at:

- Events and how they are portrayed
- Characters, their views, and how they are portrayed
- Key images repeated in the language

KNOWLEDGE

Walton, Victor and the monster all begin their stories by expressing a deep desire to explain mysteries. Each character has a different focus:

- The monster wants to 'discover the motives' (p. 117) behind the De Laceys' behaviour and to 'unravel the mystery' (p. 115) of language. His humble aims are human, social, and arise from necessity.

- Victor and Walton have lofty ambitions and are prepared to sacrifice human relationships in order to fulfil them. Victor's 'eager desire' (p. 39) to find the 'secrets of nature' (p. 41) and Walton's 'ardent' passion to explore 'a part of the world never before visited' (p. 16) take them away from their loved ones into isolation.

THEME TRACKER (A01)

Knowledge

- Vol. One, Ch. II, p. 38: Victor develops a 'thirst for knowledge'.

- Vol. One, Ch. IV, p. 54: Victor comments on the dangers of acquiring knowledge.

- Vol. Two, Ch. V, p. 123: the monster describes knowledge as 'strange'.

- When he realises he is 'a monster', the creature laments, 'Of what a strange nature is knowledge! It clings to the mind … like a lichen on the rock' (p. 123). Although the monster has learned much that is of value, Shelley is suggesting that certain kinds of knowledge can be destructive.

Throughout her novel, Shelley makes several allusions to myths about the obsessive pursuit of dangerous knowledge and its devastating consequences.

AMBITION

The central concern of the book is the moral consequences of ambition. Walton and Victor may have good intentions to confer on mankind an 'inestimable benefit' (p. 16) by discovering great things, but they fall victim to their uncontrollable desire to realise their dreams.

Both characters are only partially aware of their surroundings and what they are doing:

- Victor is only able to see with hindsight that his experiments on corpses are immoral and 'unhallowed acts' (p. 189).
- Walton's fantasy that 'snow and frost are banished' (p. 15) from the North Pole is shown in stark contrast to the facts.

Real problems occur when the ambitions of Victor and Walton endanger the lives of other people:

- Unlike Victor, Walton abandons his 'mad schemes' (p. 215), which are putting the lives of his crew at risk.
- Victor, however, is so wrapped up in the process of making his creature, that he fails even to consider what his responsibilities towards it will be once it comes alive or what the results of unleashing a gigantic monster into the world might be.

PREJUDICE

There are many examples in the book of characters who are prejudged, misunderstood and victimised by others, which leads to their rejection, isolation and despair. Shelley presents the reader with instances of officials who crassly abuse their authority and of crowds who jump to conclusions rather than evaluate the evidence before them:

- Justine is tormented by the crowd because they have already labelled her a child-murderer.
- She is wrongly put to death by judges who 'had rather ten innocent should suffer than that one guilty should escape' (p. 87). She is also forced by a priest to make a false confession.
- The Turk is condemned to death because the French authorities dislike his race, values and culture, which are different from their own.
- Victor is treated roughly and brought in front of a magistrate by the suspicious Irish crowd because he is foreign.
- The monster is beaten by the villagers because of his ugly physical appearance. They do not judge him by his actions or seek to understand him.
- Victor is also guilty of prejudice towards his creation. Until Volume One, Chapter II, the reader sees the monster as a 'devil' (p. 102) because this is how Victor sees him, but when the monster speaks, his thoughts are subtle and beautifully expressed.

THEME TRACKER A01

Ambition

- Vol. One, Letter I, pp. 16–17: Walton is ambitious about his voyage north.
- Vol. One, Ch. II, p. 42: Victor states his ambitions.
- Vol. Three, Ch. VII, p. 214: Victor tells Walton how his once 'lofty' ambitions are now 'sunk'.

THEME TRACKER A01

Prejudice

- Vol. One, Ch. VIII, p. 86: Victor perceives that the crowd seem prejudiced against Justine.
- Vol. Two, Ch. VI, p. 125: the Turkish merchant is a victim of prejudice and discrimination.
- Vol. Two, Ch. VIII, pp. 143–4: the monster encounters prejudice because of his appearance.

TOP TIP (A02)

Consider what the monster's hovel represents. It is both his prison and his vantage point on human activity, and functions as a symbol of his social exclusion, rejection and isolation.

AIMING HIGH: COMMENT ON SYMBOLS AND THEMES ⭐

Windows in the novel can be viewed symbolically. When the monster appears at Victor's window and witnesses the destruction of his new creation, the window symbolises the barriers that exist between them. The window can also be a powerful symbol of loneliness and exclusion. For example, the monster is able to observe the De Laceys through 'a small and almost imperceptible chink' (p. 110) in a boarded-up window. Windows are also a reminder that all characters have a partial and limited perspective and are prone to misunderstanding situations, making the reader play an active part in interpreting the novel's events. Can you think of something else in the novel that has symbolic importance and write a short paragraph that makes connections to some of the novel's key themes?

THEME TRACKER (A01)

Justice

● Vol. One, Ch. VIII, p. 83: Victor views Justine's trial as a 'wretched mockery of justice'.

● Vol. Two, Ch. VI, pp. 125–7: Felix fights for justice on behalf of Safie and her father.

● Vol. Three, Ch. IV, pp. 179–82: Victor is falsely accused of Henry Clerval's murder.

JUSTICE

Justine, the monster, the Turkish merchant and Victor are all suspected of crimes. Mary Shelley criticises the unfairness and corruption of the justice system, particularly in its sentencing to death of the innocent Justine.

The monster knows he has been the victim of injustice at the hands of human beings and wants Victor to correct these wrongs. He sees himself as Victor's son when he says, 'I am thy creature: I ought to be thy Adam, but I am rather the fallen angel' (p. 103), and demands that Victor fulfil his 'duty' (p. 102) as a father.

Victor recognises that he has 'no right' (p. 149) to withhold the gift of a female creature and that it would be 'justice' to create her (p. 150). To deny the monster a mate is to deny him his natural right to fraternity.

COMPANIONSHIP AND LONELINESS

THEME TRACKER (A01)

Companionship and loneliness

● Vol. One, Letter II, p. 19: Walton wishes for a friend.

● Vol. Two, Ch. IV, pp. 117–18: the monster dreams of becoming the De Lacey family's friend.

● Vol. Three, Ch. VII, p. 214: Walton fears the loss of his new friend.

The need for love, whether from friends, family or a partner, is a crucial issue in the novel.

● Walton's need for a friend, in evidence from the beginning of the novel, is met when he rescues and cares for Victor and listens to his tale.

● Victor's early years are portrayed as a paradise of kinship. Unlike the monster, he does not long for love and affection because his parents 'were possessed by the very spirit of kindness and indulgence' (p. 39).

● Close relationships are depicted as a life-giving force. There are many instances of one character being rescued by the kind acts of another. Walton and Clerval both restore Victor to life and Safie's return to Felix 'infused new life into his soul' (p. 128).

● Nature is also seen as a friend with the power to lift a human out of gloom and anxiety.

TOP TIP: WRITING ABOUT VICTOR'S ISOLATION (A02)

Victor has brought a creature to life but thereafter he fails to act as its friend, isolating the monster. Victor too is affected by his own isolation, initially due to his obsession with his scientific work and later because only he knows about the monster and its trail of destruction. Victor's feeling that he has 'unchained an enemy' (p. 189) among his family and friends makes him avoid them. Notice how Victor's inability to face up to his actions and tell his secret to someone affects all of his close relationships.

KEY QUOTATION: PERSUASIVE POWERS (A01)

As the novel approaches its climax in Volume III, Victor is torn between of his duty to the monster and his duty to friends, family and mankind at large. He has no hard evidence of the monster's good deeds, only of bad ones, and he begins to distrust the monster and to have doubts about his promise: 'I had before been moved by the sophisms of the being I had created; I had been struck senseless by his fiendish threats: but now, for the first time, the wickedness of my promise burst upon me' (p. 171). At first he thought he would be saving mankind from the monster if he made the creature a mate, but he changes his mind when he considers that the articulate monster might just be tricking him using 'sophisms' – arguments designed to deceive. He even tells Walton to be on his guard against the monster's 'powers of eloquence and persuasion' (p. 223), a comment Walton recalls during his encounter with the monster at the end of the book.

KEY CONTEXT (A03)

Look up Henry Fuseli's 1781 painting *The Nightmare* and compare it with the description of Elizabeth's death.

REVENGE

Ultimately the monster lives up to his name as a 'monster' and ceases to be a 'creature'. The climax of the novel is taken up with the theme of revenge. It is only by revenge and punishment that the monster can feel that some justice has been done. He evens up the score by subjecting Victor to the same despair that he has experienced all his life: he kills his friend; he sets Victor up as the suspect; Victor experiences prejudice; Victor endures imprisonment; and finally, the monster symbolically destroys Victor's female companion, Elizabeth.

THEME TRACKER (A01)

Revenge

- Vol. Two, Ch. VIII, p. 143: the monster's desire for revenge grows.

- Vol. Three, Ch. VI, p. 202: Victor desires to 'wreak a great and signal revenge' on the monster.

- Vol. Three, Ch. VII, p. 205: Victor's actions are governed by thoughts of revenge.

The novel ends with Victor and the monster in mutual pursuit and combat. We know from Shelley's diaries that she thought revenge a savage and destructive emotion and this is made clear in the monster's final speech. He declares with tragic insight that he finds his crimes and his character abhorrent. The only solution is suicide.

Mary Shelley

CONTEXTS

THE LIFE OF MARY SHELLEY

Mary Shelley was only nineteen years old when she completed *Frankenstein*, a novel that has become more famous than any other work from this period and which continues to inspire writers and filmmakers to this day.

PARENTS AND EARLY YEARS

Mary's mother, the writer and feminist pioneer Mary Wollstonecraft, died days after giving birth to Mary in 1797. Although Godwin, her father, was emotionally distant, he was a good teacher and Mary had free access to his extensive library and cultural and political connections.

1812–24 ROMANCE AND TRAGEDY

Between 1812 and 1814 Mary stayed with acquaintances of her father's in Scotland, during which time she began to write as a pastime. On returning home (aged sixteen) she met a visitor, the young poet Percy Shelley. He was married at the time but became her lover and later her husband.

In July 1814 Mary and Percy eloped to the continent, enraging their fathers. In 1815 the couple's first child, born prematurely, died. In 1816 the couple went to Switzerland where they met the poet Lord Byron and stayed at his villa. One night Byron read aloud some ghost stories and challenged his guests to a ghost story competition, inspiring Mary to start work on her novel.

In 1816 Mary's half-sister committed suicide and Percy Shelley's wife drowned herself. In 1818, their one-year-old daughter Clara died of dysentery and in 1819 their three-year-old son William died of malaria. Percy Shelley himself drowned in 1822. By 1824, with the death of Lord Byron, Mary found herself isolated and alone.

1824–51 WRITING AND MOTHERHOOD

Mary devoted her time to bringing up her only surviving child, Percy Florence Shelley, and writing for journals and magazines. She also published the second revised version of *Frankenstein* in 1831, and wrote the futuristic novel *The Last Man*. Mary Shelley died at the age of fifty-three in 1851.

SECRETS OF SCIENCE

Mary Shelley lived at a time of rapid scientific progress. One of the central preoccupations was the potential of electricity. In 1802 Galvani showed that running a current through the legs of frogs produced a twitch. In 1803, Aldini attached a battery to the corpse of a criminal: 'The jaw of the deceased began to quiver, the adjoining muscles were horribly contorted, and one eye was actually opened … the right hand was raised and clenched, and the legs and thighs set in motion.' These discoveries were discussed at Byron's villa and were a subject of great interest to Mary and Percy.

KEY CONTEXT A03

William Godwin was a philosopher, anarchist, atheist, novelist and an ex-minister of religion.

KEY CONTEXT A03

Victor Frankenstein grows up in the Swiss city of Geneva, and it was here that Mary Shelley began to write her novel.

KEY CONTEXT A03

Mary Shelley said she named Frankenstein after the American politician Benjamin Franklin (1706–90) who famously used a kite to demonstrate the power of electricity.

MYTHS AND LEGENDS

Mary Shelley alludes to many myths in the course of *Frankenstein*:

PROMETHEUS

There are two versions of the myth of Prometheus. In the Greek version he steals fire from the gods and gives it to humanity, but is then eternally punished by the gods. In the Latin version, he creates man from clay and water. Victor is a 'Modern Prometheus' because he rebels against the laws of nature by making an unnatural man to benefit mankind but is punished for his efforts by his creation.

FAUSTUS (OR FAUST)

Dr Faustus is an academic who turns to magic because he wants to know the secrets of the universe. He sells his soul to Satan in exchange for this knowledge but does not know what to do with his power. Tormented by the deal, he eventually perishes in hell. Similarly, Frankenstein relinquishes his family for the pursuit of knowledge and, working in isolation, creates a creature that he abandons. The monster avenges himself, like a devil, by destroying Victor's family and friends.

THE FALL OF MAN

In the Book of Genesis, Adam and Eve are forbidden by God to eat from the tree of knowledge. Tempted by Satan, they rebel. They become aware of their own sexuality and are eventually banished from the Garden of Eden. Similarly, Victor's childhood is like paradise but he is seduced by knowledge in adulthood. He rebels by creating an unnatural man. The monster also becomes aware of his own 'fallen' state when he sees his reflection.

PARADISE LOST

This epic poem written by John Milton in the 1660s tells the story of how Satan was banished from heaven by God for leading a rebellion. Satan decides to avenge himself by seducing Adam and Eve into evil and disobedience.

ROMANTICISM AND THE GOTHIC

Frankenstein is often considered a Romantic novel. Romanticism focuses on the expression of the imagination, intense feelings and the sublime power of nature. Romantics believed that art should have important themes that could arouse emotional exhilaration in the audience. The Gothic novel was an offshoot of Romanticism. The uncanny events, stormy dark settings, satanic imagery and themes of revenge and pursuit are some of *Frankenstein*'s Gothic features.

SETTINGS

Characters are described travelling over vast expanses of land. Most scenes outside are barren, wild, or desolate: the North Pole, the Mer de Glace, the peaks of the Alps, the Orkney islands. These often symbolise the separation of a character from his fellow beings. They also reflect the Romantic taste for the sublime in nature. By contrast, characters often occupy enclosed spaces: Victor's workshop at the top of his house, his dilapidated hut in the Orkneys, the prisons, the monster's hovel, Walton's cabin. These are symbols of mental as well as physical imprisonment.

KEY CONTEXT A03

Prometheus's punishment was to be chained to a cliff, where an eagle pecked daily at his liver. Percy Bysshe Shelley wrote a famous drama called *Prometheus Unbound* in 1818–19.

KEY CONTEXT A03

Christopher Marlowe, a contemporary of Shakespeare, and another great Romantic writer, Goethe, both wrote plays about Faust.

KEY CONTEXT A03

Horace Walpole's *The castle of Otranto* (1764) is generally regarded as the first Gothic novel.

Arctic

Evian

Belrive, Geneva

Irish prison

Ingolstadt

The Orkney Islands

The Alps

De Lacey cottage

PROGRESS AND REVISION CHECK

SECTION ONE: CHECK YOUR KNOWLEDGE

1 What does Walton 'bitterly feel the want of' in his second letter?

2 Name three characters who are unjustly imprisoned in the novel.

3 In which mountain range does Victor meet the monster at the beginning of Volume Two?

4 'I ought to be thy Adam, but I am rather the fallen angel' (p. 103). To which book and character is the monster alluding?

5 In his dying words, what does Victor urge Walton to avoid?

6 Fill the gap in the monster's threat to Victor: 'I will _____ my injuries.'

7 What are the 'treasures' the monster finds with some clothes in the wood?

8 Where does Victor describe as 'hardly more than a rock … continually beaten upon by the waves'?

9 Where does Walton encounter the monster?

10 Which three English Romantic poets are quoted in the novel?

TOP TIP **A01**

Answer these quick questions to test your basic knowledge of the themes, contexts and settings of the novel.

SECTION TWO: CHECK YOUR UNDERSTANDING

Task: How does Shelley show how the monster is changed by the prejudice he suffers? Think about:

- How the monster's thoughts, feelings and behaviour change
- The language used by Shelley to show how the monster changes

TOP TIP **A01**

This task requires more thought and a slightly longer response. Try to write at least three to four paragraphs.

PROGRESS CHECK

GOOD PROGRESS

I can:

- explain the main themes, contexts and settings in the text and how they contribute to the effect on the reader. ☐

- use a range of appropriate evidence to support any points I make about these elements. ☐

EXCELLENT PROGRESS

I can:

- analyse in detail the way themes are developed and presented across the novel. ☐

- refer closely to key aspects of context and setting and the implications they have for the writer's viewpoint, and the interpretation of relationships and ideas. ☐

FORM

STORIES WITHIN STORIES

Frankenstein can be described as a series of stories within stories. This is called Chinese box or Russian doll narration. Victor is the main narrator who tells Walton what the monster told him. Walton writes down for his sister what Victor told him. Each story is enfolded within another story: This helps the reader feel that they are going more deeply into the story; it shows that behind every story there is another story told from a different point of view.

The form of Shelley's narrative gives the text variety and realism – the letters of Walton and his manuscript of the story make the extraordinary events appear more believable for us. Victor's evidence of the letters between Felix and Safie, in turn, make Victor's story about the monster seem more credible for Walton. Walton's meeting with the monster at the end of the tale finally vindicates Victor's tale. The story cannot be reduced to a delirious fantasy of his deranged mind, although Victor's wild style might have an edge of madness.

LETTERS

Although Shelley's novel is not epistolary in form, it does contain a number of letters which serve some important functions. Elizabeth and Alphonse write two letters to Victor whose immediacy brings home to the reader as well as to Victor the shock and horror of William's murder.

Walton's sections of the story are told entirely through his letters to his sister. This creates a sense of authenticity about the entire novel since he declares himself an eyewitness to the events he describes. Furthermore, the series of letters provides a feeling of uncertainty about the future. Unlike Victor's life story, Walton is writing as events unfold without knowing what will happen next.

KEY CONTEXT **A03**

Many early novels, such as Samuel Richardson's *Clarissa* (1748), were epistolary, meaning they were written in the form of a series of letters.

TOP TIP **A02**

Always remember that an author shapes a novel to ensure that his or her purposes are communicated effectively to the reader. The author makes choices about positioning events and ideas in a particular order and decides to present them through particular forms.

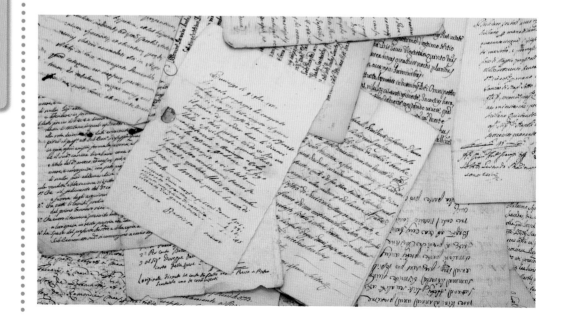

STRUCTURE

Frankenstein has an interesting structure. In effect we are reading the correspondence between Robert Walton and his sister. Like bookends, the letters start and complete 'the tale' and its 'final and wonderful catastrophe' (p. 221). In between, we hear two stories within the letters, the first from Frankenstein, the second from his creation, the monster.

HANDLING OF TIME

The events in *Frankenstein* are not told in chronological order. The novel begins after most of the action has already happened. The author returns to the past using flashbacks to explain Walton's sighting of the creature and Victor's unhealthy condition. We go back to Victor's childhood and university life, but William's murder then creates a new mystery. Shelley turns the clock back again, to the early life of the monster, to reveal the lead-up to this event. The two stories then converge. The final section explores the relationship between the creature and Victor. This brings us back full circle to the opening, but we see Walton's ship from Victor's perspective this time. The final section is the real dramatic climax to the novel where the three main characters are brought together.

> **TOP TIP** (A02)
>
> One effect of Shelley's flashback technique is to show the influence the past has on the present, how the fate of Victor and the monster are inseparable. This links to the theme of guilt: both are haunted by their past actions, which keep returning in their minds and crush their spirits.

REVISION FOCUS: MAKE CONNECTIONS ACROSS THE TEXT

As you read the novel, notice where chapters carry echoes of previous chapters. Shelley uses this device: to show how characters have been changed by events; to show how characters have not changed but are faced with a new situation; to point out similarities and/or differences between different characters' situations.

Create a table with three columns, like the one below. Use it to record any other interesting connections between chapters that you can spot.

Chapters	Connection	Detailed notes
Vol. One, Ch I and Vol Three, Ch III	They are concerned with Victor's childhood and with the monster's earliest memories.	Important difference – Victor has a loving family; the monster is alone and must learn and fend for himself. An innocence about both descriptions.

> **TOP TIP** (A02)
>
> Shelley positions events in the narrative in a way that creates drama, surprising her reader with a character's shocking change in fortune or building tension by hinting at what is to come. For example, Victor's language foreshadows the deaths of loved ones including Clerval (Vol. Three, Chapter I) and Elizabeth (Vol. Three, Chapter V).

TOP TIP: WRITING ABOUT JOURNEYS (A02)

Look at how journeys form a pattern in the narrative. Characters separate from others and return to meet them under different circumstances. Most obvious is the way the monster keeps returning to meet Victor. This creates a haunting feeling. Victor travels away from his family many times and always returns under new pressures. As an outcast, the monster is forced to journey. He also agrees to journey into exile in 'the vast wilds of South America' (p. 148) if Victor consents to make him a mate.

LANGUAGE

OVERVIEW

One of Shelley's achievements in *Frankenstein* is to make the unbelievable seem believable. The novel begins in an exciting but realistic way: an explorer looking to extend humanity's knowledge by venturing into the mysterious polar regions. Our disbelief thus suspended, we read the story with mounting amazement.

The author's choice of vocabulary and sentence structure help her to tell a fantastical story in a way that sparks her readers' imaginations and provokes thoughts and emotions in response to the novel's ideas and themes. An important idea in the novel is the double-sided nature of mankind: man is both great and terrible. These contrasts are reflected in Shelley's choice of language.

KEY CONTEXT (A03)

Coleridge, one of Mary Shelley's important influences, said that a 'willing suspension of disbelief' (*Biographia Literaria*, 1817) is an essential ingredient of fantasy.

AIMING HIGH: NARRATORIAL PERSPECTIVE ⭐

Remember that Shelley uses three **narrators** who tell their stories through their own eyes. We see the tale from different perspectives. These viewpoints are all limited and biased, which helps us to make up our own minds about the characters and explore the novel with freedom. However, this technique does have a clear effect on our feelings: we feel sympathy for Victor in the first section, change our sympathies when we meet the monster, and experience divided sympathies in the final section. How do the narrators differ in the way they recount events? Discussing the effect of the multiple narrators will enable you to gain more marks.

LANGUAGE DEVICE: ADJECTIVES AND ADVERBS

What are adjectives and adverbs?	Adjectives and adverbs modify meaning. Adjectives describe nouns or pronouns while adverbs can describe verbs, adjectives or other adverbs.
Examples	'I trembled <u>excessively</u>.' (Vol. One, Ch. V, p. 61)
	'Was man, indeed, so <u>powerful</u>, so <u>virtuous</u>, and <u>magnificent</u>, yet so <u>vicious</u> and <u>base</u>?' (Vol. Two, Ch. V, p. 122)
Effect	Example 1: The adverb suggests the intensity of Victor's trembling and the terrified feelings that inspired it.
	Example 2: This list of adjectives emphasises the extraordinary contrasts and contradictions the monster discovers as he learns about mankind.

Walton, Victor and the monster all adopt an emotional narrative style to describe their experiences; their passions are always extreme. Shelley often uses adjectives and adverbs to intensify their feelings: phrases like 'eagerly longed' (p. 116), 'frantic impulse' (p. 55) and 'tenderly love' (p. 136) add to the reader's sense that characters are experiencing extreme emotions. These dramatic descriptions of characters' feelings also help Shelley achieve and sustain a **Gothic** tone.

LANGUAGE DEVICE: IMAGERY

What is imagery?	Imagery is vivid and descriptive language that helps the reader to understand and respond to the author's meaning.
Example	Victor says that 'misfortune had tainted my mind and changed its bright visions of extensive usefulness into gloomy and narrow reflections upon self' (p. 40).
Effect	Visual imagery contrasting light with dark and looking out with looking in conveys the idea that Victor's thoughts have started to feel like a prison.

Shelley uses numerous similes and metaphors in *Frankenstein*, many of which are inspired by nature and the elements. Walton sees Victor as a 'gallant vessel' who is 'wrecked' (p. 32), overwhelmed by grander forces. Victor compares his passion for science to a 'mountain river' which 'swelling as it proceeded … became a torrent which … has swept away all my hopes and joys' (p. 40). Victor often establishes a stark contrast within a single sentence to emphasise his reversal in fortune.

LANGUAGE DEVICE: RHETORICAL TECHNIQUES

What are rhetorical techniques?	Rhetorical techniques are linguistic devices designed to have a powerful effect on the reader or listener by persuading them and/or having a strong emotional impact. Shelley uses repetition, rhetorical questions, exclamations and the contrast of opposites.
Example	The monster becomes a very eloquent speaker and uses rhetorical questions such as, 'Am I not shunned and hated by all mankind?' and 'Shall I respect man when he contemns me?' (p. 147).
Effect	The monster's questions urge Victor to understand the monster's position on an emotional and rational level.

KEY CONTEXT (A03)

When Mary Shelley wrote *Frankenstein* she set out to 'speak of the mysterious fears of our nature and awaken thrilling horror'.

Shelley uses **repetition** to build an emotional climax, for example when Victor's mind is 'filled with one thought, one conception, one purpose' (p. 49) as he resolves to return to his studies. High drama is also achieved through the use of techniques such as Walton's rhetorical question to Margaret: 'do you not feel your blood congeal with horror, like that which even curdles like mine?' (p. 202), showing his utter astonishment at what he has heard, and Victor's numerous **exclamations**, 'Abhorred monster! Fiend that thou art!' (p. 102) which add impact to his insults and accusations.

The three narrators have violent mood swings between joy and despair and Shelley's **use of opposites** emphasises these contrasts. For example, in Volume One, Victor's fascination for science in Chapter IV contrasts sharply to his reaction to Justine's trial in Chapter VIII. He is 'animated by an almost supernatural enthusiasm' (p. 52) for his work but is filled with 'heart-sickening despair' (p. 87) when he realises its consequences.

LANGUAGE DEVICE: MOTIFS

What are motifs?	Motifs are images that are repeated throughout the novel and acquire a particular resonance.
Example	Reading books plays an important part in determining several characters' destinies, making books a key motif in the novel. For example: Walton 'read nothing but our uncle Thomas's books of voyages' (p. 19) when he was a child; Victor 'chanced to find' (p. 40) books of natural philosophy; the monster reads Milton, Goethe and others.
Effect	The reader notices the impact of books on different characters' outlooks and lives. Comparisons and contrasts can be drawn, prompted by a common thread.

Other recurring motifs in *Frankenstein* are:

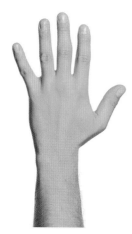

HANDS

● On several occasions characters cover their eyes with their hands when confronted with the monster. This image could suggest Victor's denial of his responsibilities, his blindness to the world around him, or his self-denial.

● We see the image of the outstretched hand, which is a symbol of the longing for human contact. We also see hands as the agents of evil: the monster's fingermarks on the necks of his victims are the dark evidence of strangulation.

LIFE AND DEATH

● Characters are restored to life by the kind actions of other human beings Shelley was aware of contemporary scientific debates about a human life force: many references are made to the human 'spirit' (p. 35) and to an 'animated' appearance (p. 119). These images contrast with the apparent death-in-life gloom of Victor who wanders 'like an evil spirit' (p. 93) and 'a restless spectre' (p. 174).

THE MOON AND STORMS

● The moon is strongly related to the presence of the monster. It is described when the monster is created and is the first object in his world that gives him pleasure. It has a more eerie effect when it appears after the monster has promised revenge.

● Storms occur frequently and create a sense of foreboding and chaos. They add to the tense Gothic atmosphere. These may be a symbol of the wild and chaotic emotions of the three main characters.

AIMING HIGH: IRONY

Shelley's use of irony and dramatic irony abound in the novel. She uses irony to help the readers take a critical attitude towards the narrators. Shelley does not interfere directly with the narrative but points out contradictions, denials and hypocrisies in her characters by using twists in the tale. Examples of irony include Victor's fatal misunderstanding of the monster's threat about his wedding night and his inconsistent views on ambition as expressed to Walton and his crew. Can you think of other examples?

PROGRESS AND REVISION CHECK

SECTION ONE: CHECK YOUR KNOWLEDGE

1. What is Victor referring to when he says, 'I would not that a mutilated one should go down to posterity' (p. 213)?

2. Which character's section of narration begins, 'It is with considerable difficulty that I remember the original era of my being'?

3. Which two adjectives does Walton use to describe Victor's 'story' (p. 32)

4. What kind of imagery is Victor using in 'demoniacal' and 'a thing such as even Dante could not have conceived' (p. 59)?

5. 'What a divine day!' (p. 197) and 'That is also my victim!' (p. 221) are examples of which rhetorical technique?

6. How does Victor learn about his brother's murder?

7. What parallel can be drawn between Volume One, Chapter V and Volume Three, Chapter III?

8. Where does Victor describe as 'belonging to another earth'?

9. 'I was passionately fond of reading.' Which of Walton's words is an adverb?

10. Whose death in Volume Three, Chapter VI is foreshadowed in Volume One, Chapter V?

TOP TIP A01

Answer these quick questions to test your basic knowledge of the form, structure and language of the novel.

SECTION TWO: CHECK YOUR UNDERSTANDING

Task: To what extent does Shelley draw parallels between Victor, Walton and the monster and the situations they face? Think about:

- Parallels between all three characters
- Key differences between them

TOP TIP A01

This task requires more thought and a slightly longer response. Try to write at least two to three paragraphs.

PROGRESS CHECK

GOOD PROGRESS

I can:

- explain how Priestley uses form, structure and language to develop the action, show relationships and develop ideas. ❑

- use relevant quotations to support the points I make, and make reference to the effect of some language choices. ❑

EXCELLENT PROGRESS

I can:

- analyse in detail Shelley's use of particular forms, structures and language techniques to convey ideas, create characters and evoke mood or setting. ❑

- select from a range of evidence, including apt quotations, to infer the effect of particular language choices and to develop wider interpretations. ❑

TOP TIP (A01)

You might also be asked to 'refer closely to', which means picking out specific examples from the text, or to focus on 'methods and techniques', which means the 'things' Shelley does, for example, the use of a particular language feature, an ironic comment on an event, etc.

UNDERSTANDING THE QUESTION

For your exam, you will be answering an extract-based question and/or a question on the whole of *Frankenstein*. Check with your teacher to see what sort of question you are doing. Whatever the task, questions in exams will need **decoding.** This means highlighting and understanding the key words so that the answer you write is relevant.

BREAK DOWN THE QUESTION

Pick out the **key words** or phrases. For example:

> Read the text from Volume One, Chapter II, 'The untaught peasant beheld the elements around him' to 'till an accident again changed the current of my ideas.'

Question: How does Shelley **present attitudes** towards **science and discovery** in **this extract** and in the **novel as a whole**?

What does this tell you?

● Focus on **the themes of science and discovery** but also on **'attitudes'** – so **different characters'** views on it.

● The word **'present'** tells you that you should focus on the ways Shelley reveals these attitudes, i.e. the techniques she uses.

● The phrases **'this extract'** and **'novel as a whole'** mean you need to **start** with the given **extract** and then **widen your discussion** to the rest of the novel, but sticking to the theme **in both**.

PLANNING YOUR ANSWER

It is vital that you generate ideas quickly and plan your answer efficiently when you sit the exam. Stick to your plan and, with a watch at your side, tick off each part as you progress.

STAGE 1: GENERATE IDEAS QUICKLY

Very briefly **list your key ideas** based on the question you have **decoded**. For example, in this **extract**:

● *Shelley presents Victor's frustration and impatience to know more*
● *Victor's interest is obsessive and possibly dangerous*
● *Victor dreams of doing good by making scientific advances*

In the **novel as a whole**:

● *The attitudes of Victor's university professors*
● *How the monster's creation alters Victor's attitude to science*
● *The parallels with Walton's hopes and ambitions for his expedition*

STAGE 2: JOT DOWN USEFUL QUOTATIONS (OR KEY EVENTS)

For example, from the **extract**:

'I was left to struggle with a child's blindness, added to a student's thirst for knowledge' (p. 42)

From the **novel as a whole**:

Volume Two, Chapter I, 'I had been the author of unalterable evils' (p. 95)

STAGE 3: PLAN FOR PARAGRAPHS

Use paragraphs to plan your answer. For example:

Paragraph	Point
Paragraph 1	**Introduce** the **argument** you wish to make: *In this extract, Shelley presents Victor's growing obsession with the idea of making important scientific discoveries. This contrasts with his horrified reaction to the monster and to the many dreadful consequences of its creation.*
Paragraph 2	Your first point: *Victor's attitude to science is at first ambitious and impulsive. He is eager to do more than 'dissect, anatomise and give names'.*
Paragraph 3	Your second point: *Victor dreams of discovering 'the elixir of life'. Ironically, he thinks only of the good that might come from such a discovery.*
Paragraph 4	Your third point: *Following the storm in Belrive, Victor becomes interested in 'electricity and galvanism' and feels disdain for his former enthusiasms. A meeting with a university lecturer reawakens Victor's ambition to 'become really a man of science, and not merely a petty experimentalist'.*
Paragraph 5	Your fourth point: *It does not take long for Victor's dreams of making scientific discoveries that are 'to the solid advantage of mankind' to turn into nightmares. With the deaths of William and Justine comes the realisation that 'I had been the author of unalterable evils'.* (You may want to add further paragraphs if you have time.)
Conclusion	**Sum up** your argument: *The boyhood dreams of both Victor and Walton continue into both men's adult years. Shelley conveys the idea that, however alluring, exploring the new and unknown can be selfish and dangerous.*

TOP TIP A02

When discussing Shelley's language, make sure you refer to the techniques she uses and, most importantly, the *effect* of those techniques. Don't just say, 'Shelley uses lots of adjectives and adverbs here'; write, 'Shelley's use of adjectives and adverbs shows/ demonstrates/ conveys the idea that ...'.

RESPONDING TO WRITERS' EFFECTS

The two most important assessment objectives are **AO1** and **AO2**. They are about *what* writers do (the choices they make, and the effects these create), *what* your ideas are (your analysis and interpretation) and *how* you write about them (how well you explain your ideas).

ASSESSMENT OBJECTIVE 1

What does it say?	What does it mean?	Dos and Don'ts
Read, understand and respond to texts. Students should be able to: ● Maintain a critical style and develop an informed personal response ● Use textual references, including quotations, to support and illustrate interpretations	You must: ● Use some of the literary terms you have learned (correctly!) ● Write in a professional way (not a sloppy, chatty way) ● Show that you have thought for yourself ● Back up your ideas with examples, including quotations	**Don't write …** *The monster is really ugly. Shelley uses horrible words to describe him.* **Do write …** *Shelley's first description of the monster's appearance conveys Victor's horror at seeing the 'dull' and 'shrivelled' body parts that he has stitched together come to life. It is as if the reader is looking through Victor's eyes, 'unable to endure the aspect of the being'.*

IMPROVING YOUR CRITICAL STYLE

Use a variety of words and phrases to show effects:

Shelley *suggests …, conveys …, implies …, presents how …, explores …, demonstrates …, describes how …, shows how …*

I/we (as readers) *infer …, recognise …, understand …, question …, see …, are given …, reflect …*

For example, look at these two alternative paragraphs by different students about Elizabeth. Note the difference in the quality of expression:

Student A:

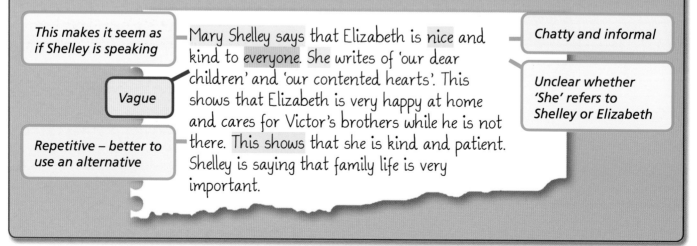

This makes it seem as if Shelley is speaking

Vague

Repetitive – better to use an alternative

Mary Shelley says that Elizabeth is nice and kind to everyone. She writes of 'our dear children' and 'our contented hearts'. This shows that Elizabeth is very happy at home and cares for Victor's brothers while he is not there. This shows that she is kind and patient. Shelley is saying that family life is very important.

Chatty and informal

Unclear whether 'She' refers to Shelley or Elizabeth

Student B:

Fits with the idea of the overall way Elizabeth is shown

Good variety of vocabulary

Phrase allows the student to explore the idea rather than state it as fact

Shelley presents Elizabeth as a kind, modest and virtuous figure when she writes to Victor in Chapter VI. She demonstrates her parental attitude towards Ernest and William with the affectionate phrase 'our dear children'. The adjectives 'placid' and 'contented' imply that she places domestic happiness above worldly ambition. Shelley also seems to be suggesting that despite her anxiety about Victor's welfare, she wishes to reassure him calmly that all is well and to wait patiently for his return.

Clear and precise language

Clear and precise language

Looks beyond the obvious and infers meaning with personal interpretation

ASSESSMENT OBJECTIVE 2

What does it say?	What does it mean?	Dos and don'ts
Analyse the language, form and structure used by the writer to create meanings and effects, using relevant subject terminology where appropriate.	'Analyse' – comment **in detail** on **particular aspects** of the text or language. 'Language' – vocabulary, imagery, variety of sentences, dialogue/speech etc. 'Form' – **how** the story is told (e.g. first person narrative, letters, diaries, chapter by chapter) 'Structure' – the **order** in which events are revealed, or in which characters appear, or **descriptions** are presented. 'create meaning' – what can we, as readers, **infer** from what the writer tells us? What is **implied** by particular descriptions, or events? 'Subject terminology' – **words** you should use when **writing** about novels, such as 'character', 'protagonist', 'imagery', 'setting' etc.	**Don't write…** *The writing is really descriptive in this bit so you could really imagine Victor and the monster in the mountains.* **Do write…** *Shelley **conveys** how the Alpine **setting** comforts and inspires Victor as he observes 'the unstained snowy mountain-top, the glittering pinnacle … the eagle, soaring amidst the clouds'. The **symbolism** of 'mountain-top', 'pinnacle' and 'soaring' are **ironic**, reminding the reader of the rapid deterioration in Victor's fortunes.*

THE THREE 'I'S

- The best analysis focuses on specific ideas or events, or uses of language and thinks about what is **implied**.

- This means drawing **inferences**. On the surface, Victor's description of his childhood tells us how happy and loving it was, and how fortunate he was to have had this kind of upbringing, but what deeper ideas does it signify about Victor's emerging character and temperament, about ambition, books and education?

- From the inferences you make across the text as a whole, you can arrive at your own **interpretation** – a sense of the bigger picture, a wider evaluation of a person, relationship or idea.

USING QUOTATIONS

One of the secrets of success in writing exam essays is to use quotations **effectively**. There are five basic principles:

1. Only quote what is most useful.
2. Do not use a quotation that repeats what you have just written.
3. Put quotation marks, e.g. ' ', around the quotation.
4. Write the quotation exactly as it appears in the original.
5. Use the quotation so that it fits neatly into your sentence.

EXAM FOCUS: USING QUOTATIONS

A01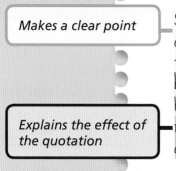

Quotations should be used to develop the line of thought in your essay and 'zoom in' on key details, such as language choices. The example below shows a clear and effective way of doing this:

Makes a clear point	Shelley presents the De Lacey family as kind and hard-working people. The monster says that 'The more I saw of them, the greater became my desire to claim their protection and kindness'. Shelley shows the reader that the monster has a sincere wish to be like them and to become their friend.
Explains the effect of the quotation	

Gives an apt quotation

However, really **high-level responses** will go further. They will make an even more precise point, support it with an even more appropriate quotation, focus in on particular words and phrases and explain the effect or what is implied to make a wider point or draw inferences. Here is an example:

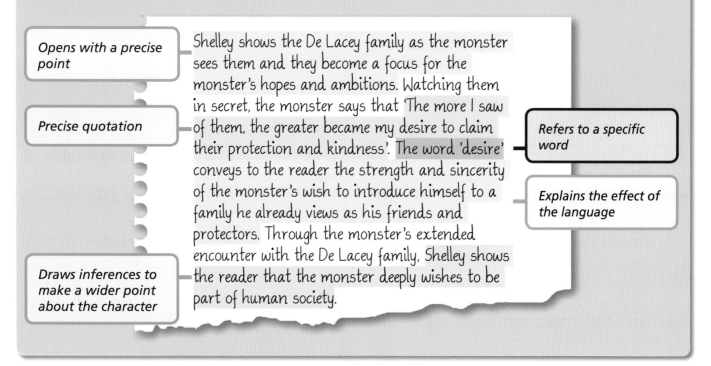

Opens with a precise point

Precise quotation

Shelley shows the De Lacey family as the monster sees them and they become a focus for the monster's hopes and ambitions. Watching them in secret, the monster says that 'The more I saw of them, the greater became my desire to claim their protection and kindness'. The word 'desire' conveys to the reader the strength and sincerity of the monster's wish to introduce himself to a family he already views as his friends and protectors. Through the monster's extended encounter with the De Lacey family, Shelley shows the reader that the monster deeply wishes to be part of human society.

Refers to a specific word

Explains the effect of the language

Draws inferences to make a wider point about the character

SPELLING, PUNCTUATION AND GRAMMAR

SPELLING

Remember to spell correctly the **author's** name, the names of all the **characters**, and the names of **places**.

A good idea is to list some of the key spellings you know you sometimes get wrong *before* the exam starts. Then use it to check as you go along. Sometimes it is easy to make small errors as you write but if you have your key word list nearby you can check against it.

PUNCTUATION

Remember:

- Use **full stops and commas in sentences accurately to make clear points**. Don't write long, rambling sentences that don't make sense; equally, avoid using a lot of short repetitive ones. Write in a fluent way, using linking words and phrases, and use **inverted commas** for **quotations**.

Don't write	Do write
Henry is very loyal to Victor turning up to help him in his hour of need such as just after the monster has come to life and also to accompany Victor on his travels in Britain before Victor's marriage to Elizabeth.	*Victor does not share his dark secret with anyone, so Clerval is no more able to help his friend with the cause of his problems than Elizabeth or Alphonse. However he, like them, worries about Victor and supports and helps him his family in a variety of ways.*

GRAMMAR

When you are writing about the text, make sure you:

- Use the present tense for discussing what the writer does, e.g. *Shelley shows the reader how and why the monster becomes an ostracised and vengeful figure.*
- Use pronouns and references back to make your writing flow.

Don't write	Do write
Despite the monster's attempt to offer help to the young girl in the woods, the monster's behaviour towards the young girl was misinterpreted and the monster was shot at by a rustic.	*Despite the monster's attempt to offer help to the 'young girl' in the woods, **his** behaviour towards **her is** misinterpreted and **he is** shot at by a 'rustic'.*

TOP TIP (A04)

Remember that spelling, punctuation and grammar is worth **approximately 5%** of your overall marks, which could mean the difference between one grade and another.

TOP TIP (A04)

Practise your spellings of key literary terms you might use when writing about the text such as: ironic, Gothic, simile, metaphor, imagery, protagonist, antagonist, character, theme, tragic etc.

TOP TIP (A04)

Enliven your essay by varying the way your sentences begin. For example, *Victor becomes a suspect in a murder case in circumstances that remind the reader of Justine's predicament in Volume One,* can also be written as: *In circumstances that remind the reader of Justine's predicament in Volume One, Victor becomes a suspect in a murder case.*

ANNOTATED SAMPLE ANSWERS

This section will provide you with three **sample responses**, one at **mid** level, one at **good** level and one at a **very high** level.

> **Question**: In Volume One, Chapter V, Victor describes the monster's appearance and movements and his own reaction. Read from 'I started from my sleep' to 'a black and comfortless sky.'
>
> Starting with this extract, write about how Shelley presents the monster and people's reactions to him.
>
> Write about:
>
> ● how Shelley describes the monster, and Victor's reaction to him in this extract
>
> ● how Shelley presents the monster's and other people's reactions to him elsewhere in the novel.

SAMPLE ANSWER 1

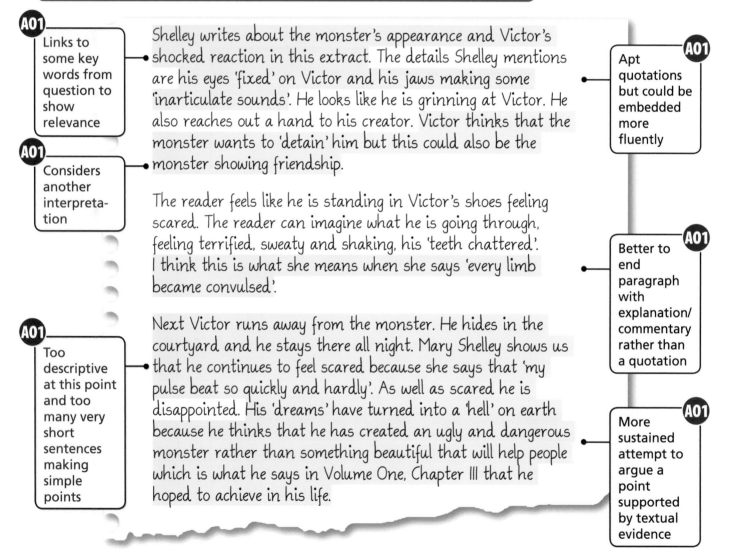

AO1 Links to some key words from question to show relevance

AO1 Considers another interpretation

Shelley writes about the monster's appearance and Victor's shocked reaction in this extract. The details Shelley mentions are his eyes 'fixed' on Victor and his jaws making some 'inarticulate sounds'. He looks like he is grinning at Victor. He also reaches out a hand to his creator. Victor thinks that the monster wants to 'detain' him but this could also be the monster showing friendship.

AO1 Apt quotations but could be embedded more fluently

The reader feels like he is standing in Victor's shoes feeling scared. The reader can imagine what he is going through, feeling terrified, sweaty and shaking, his 'teeth chattered'. I think this is what she means when she says 'every limb became convulsed'.

AO1 Better to end paragraph with explanation/commentary rather than a quotation

AO1 Too descriptive at this point and too many very short sentences making simple points

Next Victor runs away from the monster. He hides in the courtyard and he stays there all night. Mary Shelley shows us that he continues to feel scared because she says that 'my pulse beat so quickly and hardly'. As well as scared he is disappointed. His 'dreams' have turned into a 'hell' on earth because he thinks that he has created an ugly and dangerous monster rather than something beautiful that will help people which is what he says in Volume One, Chapter III that he hoped to achieve in his life.

AO1 More sustained attempt to argue a point supported by textual evidence

A03 Simple reference to context

The word 'hell' is a reference to the Bible and it is one of several words used in the novel that convey Victor's terror that he has released something awful and evil into the world. In this extract Shelley also uses 'demoniacal' (comparing the monster to a devil), 'wretch' and 'monster'. These words suggest the monster's ugly appearance and Victor's feeling that the monster is a threat to him and others.

A02 Explicit references to language choices and effects

A04 Overused word, more variety needed

The idea that the monster can do terrible things will be shown later in the novel with the deaths of William and Elizabeth and others. But Shelley also shows her readers that the monster could have turned out differently. In the monster's bit of the story about his earliest memories in Volume Two, he is shown to be a peaceful character who wants to make friends with other humans like the De Lacey family. He becomes a victim of prejudice, for example when he is attacked when he is trying to rescue a girl.

A01 Helpful example from elsewhere in novel

A02 Implicit reference to novel's form/use of multiple narrators

In this extract Shelley shows us the monster through Victor's scared and disappointed eyes. But later in the novel, the monster tells his own story and I think there is another side to the monster. However his 'hideous' appearance means people are scared of him and prejudiced against him. This is what turns him into a monster inside as well as out.

MID LEVEL

Comment
Good points are expressed about the extract and some relevant points are made about the monster in other parts of the novel. Relevant quotations are provided and there are some references to the writer's effects and purpose.

For a Good Level:

- Develop a more fluent writing style.
- Make greater reference to the effects of language, structure and form.
- Provide more detailed explanations showing deeper understanding.
- Construct the argument more confidently.

SAMPLE ANSWER 2

A01 Useful attempt to place the extract in context – shows good understanding

This extract follows an earlier passage of description about the monster's first 'convulsive' movements. This passage tells the reader a little more about the monster's appearance but focuses more on how Victor reacts to the monster.

A02 Attempt to develop personal interpretation but rather limited

At the beginning of this passage, Victor has been sleeping fitfully. Awaking from a terrible nightmare, he feels a 'cold dew' on his forehead, his teeth 'chattered' and 'every limb convulsed'. The word 'convulsed' echoes Shelley's use of the word 'convulsive' earlier in the chapter. Perhaps Shelley is reminding the reader that these two living beings have more in common than Victor seems to realise.

A02 Close analysis of language

Shelley's descriptions of both Victor and the monster are very powerful and dramatic. Details like the 'dim and yellow light of the moon' and comparisons with a 'mummy' and with creatures from Dante's *Inferno* create a mood of horror and make the reader imagine visual scenes that are very typical of Gothic horror. The way the monster's eyes are 'fixed' on Victor and the way he stretches out his hand are frightening and make the reader think that the monster might pursue Victor however hard he tries to hide.

A01 Interesting interpretation, could be expressed more powerfully

A03 Point about context made in connection to the text

This image of the monster is everyone's first impression of the monster – resulting in prejudice. The villagers who attack the monster in Volume Two, Chapter III are examples of this prejudice; their 'children shrieked, and one of the women fainted' because of the monster's appearance. But underneath his ugliness, Shelley shows the reader later in the novel that the monster is capable of fine words and fine feelings. Examples of this include his response to nature in Volume Two, Chapter III and the intelligence he shows in relation to literary texts in Volume Two, Chapter VII. In Volume Two, Chapter IV the monster sees for himself his 'miserable deformity' and is 'terrified' just like Victor and all other humans who see him. But Shelley shows us that behind this exterior, the monster wishes to be part of society not to terrorise it and his educated way of explaining things leaves the reader with more understanding of the monster.

A01 Too vague - needs to be explained in more detail with supporting evidence

A01 Appropriate textual evidence supplied to support comments

A01 Elegant, more 'conceptualised' expression of ideas

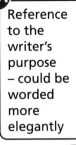

A01

Reference to the writer's purpose – could be worded more elegantly

Shelley seems to suggest that as soon as Victor brings his creation to life - something he had long dreamed of doing - his view of that creation and of that achievement are spoiled. It is 'only when those muscles and joints were rendered capable of motion' that Victor seems to realise that all his hard work has ended not gloriously but with 'disappointment'. At the end of the extract he comments that 'the change was so rapid, the overthrow so complete!' This exclamation reflects Victor's highly emotional and nervous state of mind and also implies that Victor realises that his contented life and promising career have come to an end, and that things will never be the same again.

A02

Precise comment about a language technique and its effects

GOOD LEVEL

Comment

There is plenty of interpretation of the text here and points are supported by relevant evidence. There is some analysis of language and an attempt to understand the extract in the context of the chapter from which it comes and in the context of the novel as a whole though the latter could be developed further.

For a High Level:

- Provide a more sustained analysis of text and ideas.
- Develop a coherent overall argument, expressed fluently and elegantly.
- Make more links between close analysis and wider themes, effects of structure and form, etc.
- Demonstrate more of a sense of the writer at work.

SAMPLE ANSWER 3

A01 Confident assertion of interpretation

A02 Secure handling of novel's structure and linking of key events

A01 Wide-ranging textual examples provided

A01 In-depth look at key themes of novel

In this extract, the reader sees that Victor's view of his newly animated creation is already one that sees the monster as a threat and himself as a potential victim. The words and phrases 'horror', 'hell' and 'a thing such as ever Dante could not have conceived' are intensely powerful and dramatic words that show that Victor believes he has unleashed an evil being of great magnitude into the world. Through Victor's eyes, the two characters are strongly contrasted - the 'mortal' protagonist versus a 'demoniacal' antagonist or foe. Victor's nightmare, the reference to the 'dim and yellow light of the moon' and Victor's description of the monster as a 'corpse' who might 'approach' him all contribute to the Gothic horror of the scene. The use of such language and recurrent Gothic motifs anticipates Victor's terrifying encounters with the monster later in the novel - in the Alps, on the Orkneys and in Evian.

However, it is clear that Victor does not give a thought to the being he has created beyond the immediate consequences of the monster's existence for his own safety and wellbeing. The monster appears to grin, makes sounds and reaches out a hand 'seemingly to detain me' and all of these behaviours are interpreted by Victor to be fearful and menacing. Although they could be interpreted as more amicable in their intention, it is only Victor's perspective that the reader is shown. Of course Victor is not alone in responding to the sight of the monster in this way; the villagers, the De Lacey children, even the monster himself are appalled by the monster's 'miserable deformity' and treat even his acts of kindness with the greatest suspicion.

Rather than feeling a sense of duty towards the creature he has created, Victor runs away from him, an example of the prejudice and irresponsibility (leading to neglect or abandonment) that Shelley writes about in relation to numerous characters in her novel. In the extract, Victor hides from the monster 'in the courtyard belonging to the house' and remains there all night. This episode may be seen to foreshadow the monster's retreat into the hovel adjoining the De Laceys' cottage in Volume 2. From his vantage point, the monster observes the family at work and leisure and grows fond of them hoping eventually to win their acceptance and

A02 Analysis of language choices and their effects

A01 Argument well supported by detailed evidence

A02 Insightful remark about novel's form and narrative perspective

A01 Elegant, fluent style

A02 Interesting analysis of structure using appropriate terminology

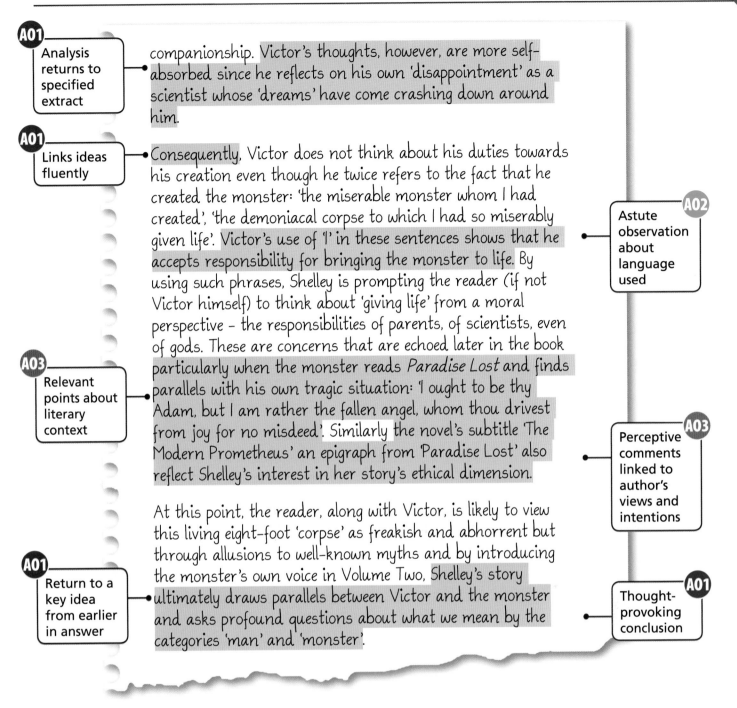

AO1 Analysis returns to specified extract

companionship. Victor's thoughts, however, are more self-absorbed since he reflects on his own 'disappointment' as a scientist whose 'dreams' have come crashing down around him.

AO1 Links ideas fluently

Consequently, Victor does not think about his duties towards his creation even though he twice refers to the fact that he created the monster: 'the miserable monster whom I had created', 'the demoniacal corpse to which I had so miserably given life'. Victor's use of 'I' in these sentences shows that he accepts responsibility for bringing the monster to life. By using such phrases, Shelley is prompting the reader (if not Victor himself) to think about 'giving life' from a moral perspective – the responsibilities of parents, of scientists, even of gods. These are concerns that are echoed later in the book particularly when the monster reads *Paradise Lost* and finds parallels with his own tragic situation: 'I ought to be thy Adam, but I am rather the fallen angel, whom thou drivest from joy for no misdeed'. Similarly the novel's subtitle 'The Modern Prometheus' an epigraph from 'Paradise Lost' also reflect Shelley's interest in her story's ethical dimension.

AO2 Astute observation about language used

AO3 Relevant points about literary context

AO3 Perceptive comments linked to author's views and intentions

At this point, the reader, along with Victor, is likely to view this living eight-foot 'corpse' as freakish and abhorrent but through allusions to well-known myths and by introducing the monster's own voice in Volume Two, Shelley's story ultimately draws parallels between Victor and the monster and asks profound questions about what we mean by the categories 'man' and 'monster'.

AO1 Return to a key idea from earlier in answer

AO1 Thought-provoking conclusion

VERY HIGH LEVEL

Comment
This answer provides a compelling exploration of text. The convincing argument is structured and expressed confidently, using detailed, focused analysis of language and extremely well-integrated comments about context. The effect of the writer's choices is paramount in the extract and is explored confidently and perceptively. The writing style is elegant and fluent.

PRACTICE TASK

Write a full-length response to this exam-style question and then use the **Mark scheme** on page 96 to assess your own response.

> **Question**: In Volume Three, Chapter V (pp. 189–90), Victor's father Alphonse is trying to understand and support his troubled son.
>
> Read from 'My father's care and attentions were indefatigable' to 'concerning the wretch I had created'.
>
> Starting with this extract, how does Mary Shelley present relationships between parents and children?
>
> Write about:
>
> ● how Shelley presents Victor's relationship with his father in this extract
> ● how Shelley presents parent–child relationships in the novel as a whole.

TOP TIP

You can use the General skills section of the **Mark scheme** on page 96 to remind you of the key criteria you'll need to cover.

Remember:

● Plan quickly and efficiently by using key words from the question.
● Write equally about the extract and the rest of the novel.
● Focus on the techniques Shelley uses and the effect of these on the reader.
● Support your ideas with relevant evidence, including quotations.

FURTHER QUESTIONS

 In Volume Two, Chapter IX, the monster asks Victor to create a companion for him.

Read from 'The being finished speaking' to 'I swear inextinguishable hatred' (pp. 147–8).

Explore the themes of friendship and loneliness by referring to this extract and to the novel as a whole.

2 In Volume Three, Chapter I, Victor writes about Henry's love of nature.

Read from 'He felt as if he had been transported' to 'the anguish which his remembrance creates' (pp. 160–62).

Write about how Mary Shelley presents Henry Clerval in this extract and about his significance in the novel as a whole.

3 'Mary Shelley's use of language in *Frankenstein* inspires dread, disgust and horror in the reader.' How far do you agree with this view? Analyse at least three passages from the novel to support your ideas.

4 Explain how Mary Shelley explores the theme of ambition in the novel.

Consider:

● the importance of ambition in the novel
● how different attitudes to it are presented.

LITERARY TERMS

allusion	an indirect reference to something, e.g. another text
ambiguity	doubt or uncertainty of meaning
ambivalent	when an author or character feels two opposite extremes of emotion at the same time
antagonist	character in opposition to the protagonist or hero
atmosphere	a setting's or situation's mood
dialogue	the words that are spoken by characters in conversation
epic poem	long narrative poem, written in elevated style about the exploits of superhuman heroes
extended metaphor	a metaphor that is introduced and then developed throughout all or part of a work of literature
flashback	when the narration jumps backward in time to an earlier point in the story
foreshadow	when an author hints at what is to come
Gothic	literature that contains supernatural, unexplained and weird events in order to provoke either terror or horror in the reader with nightmarish images. In the late eighteenth century the Gothic novel was far more popular than realism
imagery	creating a word picture; common forms are metaphors and similes
irony	saying one thing while meaning another, often through understatement, concealment or indirect statement. Dramatic irony is when the audience or reader knows something the character does not
metaphor	a figure of speech in which something, someone or an action is described as something else in order to imply a resemblance, e.g. Frankenstein is a 'gallant vessel' to Captain Walton
motif	an image, idea, or situation which recurs throughout the text forming a pattern, e.g. the association between the monster and the moon
narrative	a story or account of events, real or imagined
narrator	storyteller
protagonist	the central character of the novel or narrative
realism	writing which deals in a down-to-earth way with ordinary life
rhetorical techniques	techniques that use language effectively to persuade or to provoke an emotional response
rhetorical question	a question that is asked in order to emphasise a point rather than to receive an answer
Romantic	an influential cultural movement in literature, music and painting (in the late eighteenth and early nineteenth centuries) that focused on the expression of sublime emotions aroused by nature, the imagination, dreams and solitude
setting	the place or environment where the events in a story are set. Settings are sometimes used to create a mood, reflect a character's inner feelings, or are used symbolically
simile	a figure of speech using 'like' or 'as' to make a comparison
sublime	refers to a stimulus which arouses exalted emotions; it may be a feeling of overpowering joy or terror
symbolise	to use an image to mean or represent something else, often an idea or emotion
uncanny	eerie, a feeling created by something seemingly supernatural
unreliable narrator	a strongly biased or untrustworthy narrator

CHECKPOINT ANSWERS

CHECKPOINT 1, page 11

He believes it is a 'region of beauty and delight' (p. 15).

CHECKPOINT 2, page 13

His men are 'bold, and apparently firm of purpose' (p. 23).

CHECKPOINT 3, page 14

Walton admires Victor: he has 'extraordinary merits' and is a 'wonderful man' (p. 30).

CHECKPOINT 4, page 17

He was the father of Caroline, Victor's mother.

CHECKPOINT 5, page 20

Waldman thinks Victor has 'ability' and he has 'no doubt of [his] success' (p. 50).

CHECKPOINT 6, page 22

Victor quotes lines from Coleridge's *Rime of the Ancient Mariner* (p. 60).

CHECKPOINT 7, page 23

Justine is looked upon almost as a member of the family (pp. 66–7).

CHECKPOINT 8, page 25

He initially believes she is guilty but changes his mind once Victor assures him otherwise and then hopes for her acquittal (p. 81).

CHECKPOINT 9, page 26

They are enraged and feel Justine is guilty of 'the blackest ingratitude' (p. 86).

CHECKPOINT 10, page 28

He feels he 'ought to render him happy before [he] complained of his wickedness' (p. 104).

CHECKPOINT 11, page 32

The kindness he shows towards his children and his encouragement of them (p. 115).

CHECKPOINT 12, page 34

Her 'angelic beauty' (p. 119).

CHECKPOINT 13, page 35

She takes money and jewels and escapes from her father (p. 129).

CHECKPOINT 14, page 36

He finds Victor's papers in the pockets of the clothing he took from Victor's laboratory (p. 132).

CHECKPOINT 15, page 37

His feelings of 'kindness and gentleness' are changed to a 'hellish rage' when he is shot at (p. 143).

CHECKPOINT 16, page 38

He says that it will make him happy to see that he can 'excite the sympathy of some existing thing' (p. 148).

CHECKPOINT 17, page 40

As a father, he is keen that Victor should have a companion (p. 156).

CHECKPOINT 18, page 41

After disposing of the female monster, he falls asleep in a boat and is taken by the sea (pp. 176–7).

CHECKPOINT 19, page 42

He had been strangled: there was 'the black mark of fingers on his neck' (p. 179).

CHECKPOINT 20, page 45

He says that it will be too difficult to follow him and also that too much time has passed since he committed his crimes (p. 203).

PROGRESS AND REVISION CHECK ANSWERS

PART TWO, pages 49–50

SECTION ONE: CHECK YOUR KNOWLEDGE

1. she is his sister
2. Switzerland
3. Caroline, Alphonse, Ernest and William
4. Ingolstadt
5. natural philosophy
6. about eight feet tall
7. because it took longer to work with smaller body parts
8. black fingermarks
9. because her confessor 'threatened excommunication and hell fire'
10. 'stones and many other kinds of missile weapons'
11. guitar
12. he brings them firewood
13. speech/language
14. the Turkish merchant, from prison in Paris with his daughter Safie; to safety in Italy
15. *Paradise Lost*
16. the magistrate presiding over the case of Henry Clerval's murder
17. he thinks the monster means to attack him rather than Elizabeth
18. Villa Lavenza on the shores of Lake Como, stopping at Evian on the way
19. he will build and set fire to a pile of wood and burn to death
20. Prometheus (the novel's subtitle is 'The Modern Prometheus')

SECTION TWO: CHECK YOUR UNDERSTANDING

Task 1

- Justine is portrayed as a virtuous and stoical figure more concerned with divine justice than with the verdict of an earthly court – in contrast to the worldly ambitions of men like Frankenstein and Walton.
- Her religious faith and affection for the Frankensteins remain strong and she consoles herself that she will see 'Dear William' again in heaven (p. 88). The reader knows there has been a terrible miscarriage of justice and that she is another victim of the monster.
- For Victor, Justine's guilty verdict and execution are 'tortures' – he sees her as 'the saintly sufferer' (p. 90) and refers to himself as 'the true murderer' (p. 89).
- Victor also has to endure Elizabeth's and his father's 'grief' but cannot admit what he knows as he would be dismissed as a 'madman' (p. 90).

Task 2

- This scenery is familiar to Victor; it represents his home but is also somewhere he can be alone and forget his troubles
- He finds it restorative and 'consoling' (p. 99). Gazing at Mont Blanc, he says, 'My heart, which was before sorrowful, now swelled with something like joy' (p. 101).
- The idea of walking through beautiful, dramatic landscapes admiring 'sublime and magnificent' views is a Romantic one. Ironically, the monster has also turned to such landscapes as a place of 'refuge' (p. 103).
- The monster's sudden appearance is a dramatic interruption of Victor's enjoyment of his solitude, a reminder that he cannot escape the monster and that their destines are forever connected.

PART THREE, page 63

SECTION ONE: CHECK YOUR KNOWLEDGE

1. Elizabeth
2. Henry Clerval
3. Victor's university professors
4. De Lacey
5. the monster
6. Beaufort
7. Captain Walton
8. Ernest Frankenstein
9. She is on horseback and dressed in a dark suit with a thick black veil
10. To Justine

SECTION TWO: CHECK YOUR UNDERSTANDING

- Shelley shows how Victor's scientific ambitions started at a young age. He describes how he was 'deeply smitten with the thirst for knowledge' (p. 38).
- He uses passionate language such as 'It was the secrets of heaven and earth that I desired to learn' (p. 39) and 'the birth of that passion, which afterwards ruled my destiny' (p. 40) to convey the strength of his ambitions.
- Walton's account shows how determined Victor is to pursue the monster: 'He manifested the greatest eagerness to be upon deck' (p. 28) despite his ill health.
- Even though Victor warms Walton to 'avoid ambition' (p. 220), he also urges the crew to retain their ambition and spirit even in difficult times: 'Did you not call this a glorious expedition?' (p. 217).

PART FOUR, page 71

SECTION ONE: CHECK YOUR KNOWLEDGE

1. a friend
2. Justine, the Turkish merchant, Victor
3. Alps
4. Satan in Milton's *Paradise Lost*
5. ambition
6. revenge
7. the books *Paradise Lost*, *Plutarch's Lives* and the *Sorrows of Werter*
8. the Orkney island where he works on the monster's companion
9. in a cabin onboard his ship where Victor's dead body rests
10. Shelley, Coleridge and Wordsworth

SECTION TWO: CHECK YOUR UNDERSTANDING

- The monster has to physically retreat from view to avoid being attacked and takes 'refuge in a low hovel' (p. 109).
- He bides his time before introducing himself to De Lacey, but the reaction of the humans to his appearance is fearful and violent.
- 'Finding myself unsympathised with' (p. 138), the monster loses hope and becomes vengeful, turning to violence – arson and ultimately murder.
- In his encounter with William, he hoped that it would be possible to find someone young enough as to be 'unprejudiced' (p. 144).

PART FIVE, page 77

SECTION ONE: CHECK YOUR KNOWLEDGE

1. his narrative of events
2. the monster
3. 'strange and harrowing'
4. satanic imagery
5. exclamations
6. in a letter from his father
7. they are both chapters about the creation of a monster (but the second one is destroyed rather than brought to life)
8. the Alps
9. 'passionately'
10. Elizabeth's

SECTION TWO: CHECK YOUR UNDERSTANDING

- Victor, Walton and the monster all have ambitions and hopes – Walton's 'great purpose' (p. 17), for example – that in retrospect appear idealistic and naive.
- Their personal quests lead them 'to the northward' (p. 208) where the novel begins and ends. Shelley's choice of such a desolate setting 'almost too severe to support' (p. 208) seems fitting.
- Victor and the monster's lives converge at the end of the novel. They see their destinies as profoundly interconnected; as Victor says, he cannot 'rest' until the monster dies (p. 212).
- All suffer great despair – but what sets the monster apart from Victor and Walton is that he has no one to turn to: 'But am I not alone, miserably alone?' (p. 103). Victor and Walton have family and friends; the monster is a true outcast.

MARK SCHEME

POINTS YOU COULD HAVE MADE

- Alphonse is concerned that Victor seems to be shunning human society. He believes that human contact would help his son.

- Shelley suggests that because Alphonse 'did not know the origin' of his son's 'sufferings' (p. 189), his attempts to help him are destined to fail.

- Although they are misguided, Alphonse's 'care and attentions' are 'indefatigable' (p. 189) and forgiving. Alphonse stands by his son in times of need such as when he is accused of Henry's murder earlier in Volume Three.

- Less helpfully, in Volume One, Alphonse did not teach Victor about science and simply dismissed Agrippa as 'sad trash' (p. 40).

- Comparisons and contrasts can be drawn between Alphonse and Victor's relationship and other parent–child relationships in the novel including Safie and her father, De Lacey and his children, Henry and his father and Justine and her mother.

- The reader may also reflect on the parental nature of the relationship between Victor and the monster. Indeed, the monster accuses Victor of failing in his duties towards his creation.

GENERAL SKILLS

Make a judgement about your level based on the points you made (above) and the skills you showed.

Level	Key elements	Spelling, punctuation and grammar	Tick your level
Very high	**Very well-structured answer which gives a rounded and convincing viewpoint.** You use very detailed analysis of the writer's methods and effects on the reader, using precise references which are fluently woven into what you say. You draw inferences, consider more than one perspective or angle, including the context where relevant, and make interpretations about the text as a whole.	You spell and punctuate with consistent accuracy, and use a very wide range of vocabulary and sentence structures to achieve effective control of meaning.	
Good to High	**A thoughtful, detailed response with well-chosen references.** At the top end, you address all aspects of the task in a clearly expressed way, and examine key aspects in detail. You are beginning to consider implications, explore alternative interpretations or ideas; at the top end, you do this fairly regularly and with some confidence.	You spell and punctuate with considerable accuracy, and use a considerable range of vocabulary and sentence structures to achieve general control of meaning.	
Mid	**A consistent response with clear understanding of the main ideas shown.** You use a range of references to support your ideas and your viewpoint is logical and easy to follow. Some evidence of commenting on writers' effects, though more needed.	You spell and punctuate with reasonable accuracy, and use a reasonable range of vocabulary and sentence structures.	
Lower	**Some relevant ideas but an inconsistent and rather simple response in places.** You show you have understood the task and you make some points to support what you say, but the evidence is not always well chosen. Your analysis is a bit basic and you do not comment in much detail on the writer's methods.	Your spelling and punctuation is inconsistent and your vocabulary and sentence structures are both limited. Some of these make your meaning unclear.	